PRESENTED TO

_____

BY

_____

It Happens on Sunday

FOREWORD BY Reggie White

*Finding Courage for a
Life of Greatness*

Pat Williams
WITH Jim Denney

J. Countryman
Nashville, Tennessee

ADVANCE PRAISE FOR *IT HAPPENS ON SUNDAY*

Those of us who love to read about our favorite football players will get a chance to do that in Pat Williams' new book *It Happens on Sunday*. This book offers a unique insight into the athletes we admire—how they approach the game, how they approach life, and the factors that enable them to succeed in both.

RAYMOND BERRY, former NFL great and head coach

Being a cheerful spirit and sharing eternal truths have been Pat Williams' strengths for a long time. In *It Happens on Sunday*, he combines the urgency of the football "moment of truth" with Christian basics for a special kind of encouragement.

BILL CURRY, former NFL player and college coach

Pat Williams is a great writer! This is his best yet. When I played in the NFL for 12 years back in the 1960s, I saw football as a great platform from which to talk about my faith! This super-thrilling book carries on that tradition in a most captivating way! It's current and exciting—a must read!

BILL GLASS, former NFL defensive end

Pat Williams brings a wonderful message of success in life through spiritual values from true life experiences and the testimony of former and current NFL players.

LAMAR HUNT, founder, Kansas City Chiefs

It Happens on Sunday is a unique combination of inspirational lessons learned on the gridiron, combined with spirituality that readers can draw upon in creating a winning game plan for life.

H. WAYNE HUIZENGA, Chairman of AutoNation and owner of the Miami Dolphins

I am delighted Pat Williams has written *It Happens on Sunday*. He has laid out some powerful principles from NFL players and coaches that will make a difference in your life.

ARCHIE MANNING, former NFL quarterback

It Happens on Sunday is filled with great stories and life-changing principles from some of my favorite NFL personalities. The photographs put you right in the middle of the action. The whole package is powerful!

DON SHULA, NFL's all-time winningest coach

Throughout my career in the NFL, I kept my eye on the ultimate goal—to hear "Well done, my good and faithful servant" from my Lord and Savior, Jesus Christ. I still keep my eye on that goal. This book reveals how you, too, can achieve the ultimate reward.

MIKE SINGLETARY, former Chicago Bears linebacker

It Happens on Sunday is a powerful book about what's right about the NFL. Many players and coaches are using their influence wisely, and this book tells their story.

BART STARR, former Green Bay Packers quarterback and head coach

A great "recharge-the-battery" book! We all make tough "fourth-and-one" decisions every day, and those decisions have a real impact on our lives and the people around us. *It Happens on Sunday* gives us the insights we all need to make good decisions in pressure situations.

DAVE WANNSTEDT, head coach, Miami Dolphins

I couldn't possibly count the lessons I've learned about life and faith during the highs and lows of my football career. In reading the stories of these athletes, you, too, will begin to see how these on-field experiences can be lessons that shape the way we live.

DANNY WUERFFEL, NFL quarterback

Photo Credits:
Copyright © Joel Zwink/Zwink Photography - Cover, Back Cover, Endpapers, 23, 48-49, 61, 73, 86-87, 89, 105.
Copyright © AP/Wide World Photos - 21.
Copyright © Allsport Photography - David Leeds 1, 74; Al Bello 2-3, 28; Markus Boesch 4-5; Stephen Dunn 6-7, 25; Harry How 8-9; Craig Jones 10; Jonathan Daniel 11, 31, 36, 51, 60, 72, 91 Jamie Squire 12; Jeff Gross 15; Rick Stewart 16, 55, 107; Tom Pidgeon 19; Scott Halleran 27, 39, 63, 98, 116; Jed Jacobsohn 32; Vernon & John Biever 34; Tom Hauck 37, 110, 115, 119; Doug Pensinger 42, 104; Andy Lyons 44, 57, 120; John Swart 52; Mark Lyons 66; Otto Greule Jr 79, 95, 102; Ken Levine 81; Scott Strazzante 83; Ezra O. Shaw 84; Chris Stanford 86; Brian Bahr 92; Rich Clarkson 101.

J. Countryman® is a trademark of Thomas Nelson Inc.

Designed by Koechel-Peterson and Associates, Minneapolis, Minnesota

ISBN 0-8499-5754-0

Printed and bound in Mexico

www.thomasnelson.com

CONTENTS

DEDICATION

Dedicated with love to my
sons Stephen and Thomas,
two boys who are growing
into fine young men
as they learn and live out
the lessons of this book.

SUNDAY IS THE DAY IT ALL HAPPENS.

For the men who play the game,
and for all those who love the game,
there's no other day quite like Sunday.
That's when men explode across the line,
reaching for their goals, reaching for glory,
reaching for victory.

It's a day of INTENSITY.

A day of TRIUMPH.

A day of REJOICING.

A day when unbelievable power is unleashed
for all the world to see.

It happens on Sunday.
And it happens right **NOW!**

by Reggie White, No. 92

Foreword

*"The Minister of Defense," retired defensive end
(Philadelphia Eagles, Green Bay Packers, and
Carolina Panthers); future Hall of Famer;
Author of* In the Trenches, God's Playbook,
and Fighting the Good Fight; *and all-time
NFL sackmaster—198 career sacks!*

January 26, 1997, was the day my career became complete.

I ran out of the tunnel of the Louisiana Superdome and stepped onto the field of Super Bowl XXXI, Packers versus Patriots. The game got off to an explosive start—a 54-yard TD pass from Brett Favre to Andre Rison, then an interception and a field goal. Early in the first quarter, we led 10-0. The Patriots answered back with touchdown drives on their next two possessions. At the end of the first quarter, New England led 14-10.

Early in the second quarter, Brett hit Antonio Freeman with an 81-yard touchdown pass—the longest play from scrimmage in Super Bowl history. Then, just before halftime, Brett ran the ball into the left corner of the end zone—it was Green Bay 27, New England 14.

The halftime show featured fireworks and motorcycles, so when the second half started, the air under the dome was dense with smoke. Halfway through the third quarter, my lungs burned and my legs felt like rubber. Right after Curtis Martin ran for a touchdown, bringing the Patriots within 6, I went to our safety, Eugene Robinson, and said, "I'm tired, man, and my legs are gone! You've got to pray for me!"

Eugene quoted Isaiah 40:31. "Reggie," he said, " 'Those who wait on the Lord shall renew their strength; they shall mount up with wings like eagles, they shall run and not be weary, they shall walk and not faint.' Trust God, man, and He'll give you the strength."

Reggie White

Just after he said this, our kick returner, Desmond Howard, ran a kickoff back for a 99-yard touchdown, the longest in Super Bowl history. A 2-point conversion made it Green Bay 35, New England 21.

Back on the field, I noticed that my lungs felt good and my legs felt strong. I jumped right over Max Lane, the Patriots right tackle, and hit Drew Bledsoe just an instant after he got the ball away. *Man, I thought, Eugene was right! God has renewed my strength—big time!* Next play, I went inside on Max, clubbing him aside with my right arm, and sacked Bledsoe for 8 yards. We lined up again at third and 13. This time I beat Max around the corner and sacked Bledsoe for 6 yards. *Man, I thought, this is amazing! Just a moment ago, I could hardly stand!*

I sacked Bledsoe again in the fourth quarter and later found out that my three sacks set a new Super Bowl record. At the end of the game, the

Packers had reclaimed the NFL Championship for the first time in twenty-nine years. I knelt on the field with my Christian brothers from both teams, and we thanked God for a game cleanly played, without serious injuries.

It was an amazing privilege to win the Super Bowl. But as thrilling as that was, I can honestly say that I have experienced even greater privileges and deeper joys. It is a daily privilege to know the Lord Jesus in a personal way. It is a profound privilege to be married to a godly woman like Sara, and to be a dad to two children who love Jesus. It is an honor to be involved in ministry and to see people become spiritually renewed and economically empowered. And that is what this book is about: Football. Family. Faith in God. Caring about the community. Making a difference in the world.

I know the men who wrote this book. I first met Pat Williams when I was with the Philadelphia Eagles and he was general manager of the basketball 76ers. Pat is a committed Christian, a dedicated father to nineteen kids (four by birth, fourteen by international adoption, and one by remarriage). And I got to know Jim Denney when we worked together on my autobiography, *Reggie White—In the Trenches*.

As both a preacher and football player, I can tell you that Sundays are very special days to me. These guys have written a powerful book that will put you right where I've been on a lot of glorious Sundays—under the pads and inside the helmet. So turn the page and start reading—

And "feel the power" of *It Happens on Sunday!*

Reggie White

CHAPTER ONE
Fourth and Goal

"Do you not know that those who run in a race all run, but one receives the prize? Run in such a way that you may obtain it."

1 CORINTHIANS 9:24

*The way you
handle a crisis
reveals what
your soul is
made of.*

It's fourth and goal.

With just seconds remaining, you trail by a field goal. Just a few yards of real estate spell the difference between winning and losing. Do you kick the field goal and send the game into overtime? Or go for a touchdown? In football or in life, fourth and goal is the make-or-break situation that defines the moment and reveals what you are made of.

Case in point: Super Bowl XXVII, January 31, 1993—Jimmy Johnson's Dallas Cowboys versus Marv Levy's Buffalo Bills. It was the Bills' third consecutive Super Bowl—both previous trips had ended in losses.

In this game, two disastrous first quarter turnovers by Bills quarterback Jim Kelly had Buffalo trailing 14-7, giving Troy Aikman and the Cowboys all the momentum. But early in the second quarter, the Buffalo Bills battled back to a first-and-goal on the Dallas 4 and aimed to even the score. On first down, Buffalo fullback Carwell Gardner carried the ball up the gut for 3 yards. On second and goal, running back Thurman Thomas was stuffed for no gain and limped off the field. On third and goal, Kenneth

Pete Metzelaars

Davis scurried around the left flank but was tackled for no gain. That brought up fourth and goal on the Dallas 1.

Fourth and goal.

Bills head coach Marv Levy had a tough decision: Kick the field goal—or go for the end zone? Levy said, "Go for it."

Thurman Thomas came back on the field, and he, Gardner, and tight end Pete Metzelaars spread themselves out. Kelly took the snap and dropped back to pass. Thomas, Gardner, and Metzelaars crossed into the end zone, but a ferocious Dallas pass rush gave Kelly no time to set and throw. Hurried, he chucked the ball toward Metzelaars—

But it landed in the arms of Dallas safety Thomas Everett.

That interception became the defining moment of Super Bowl XXVII. Jim Kelly only threw one more pass in the game—an incompletion. On that play, Kelly was buried by a Dallas blitz as he released the ball. Kelly reinjured some sprained ligaments in his right knee, and his day was over.

Kelly's backup, Frank Reich, came onto the field. Reich had led the Bills to a wildcard playoff victory over the Houston Oilers just a few weeks earlier, overcoming a seemingly insurmountable 32-point deficit. Could he engineer another comeback in Super Bowl XXVII?

Reich went to work and led the Bills downfield. Soon, they were again knocking on the Cowboys' front door. It was fourth and goal at the Dallas 3. But this time, Bills head coach Marv Levy didn't say, "Go for it." He called the kicking unit onto the field. Buffalo settled for a 21-yard field goal and trailed 14-10.

And so it went. By halftime, Dallas led 28-10. After three quarters, Dallas led 31-17. During the fourth, Dallas scored three times in 2:33, sealing the blowout. As time ran out, the score was Dallas 52, Buffalo 17.

The crucial pivot point of the game was that desperate fourth-and-goal play on the Dallas 1-yard line. Frank Reich reflects, "My Christian faith has made me a better athlete because I don't feel as though I have to be controlled by my circumstances or the environment around me. It's in my faith in Jesus and the strength and hope I find in Him that I can overcome anything, on or

"Early in my career, when I wasn't a Christian, that caused a lot of problems and brought a lot of stress into our lives. Now [the uncertainty] is there, but we know that Christ is in control."

PETE METZELAARS
Former Tight End
Buffalo Bills and
Carolina Panthers

off the field. Sometimes that means overcoming a 32-point deficit. But sometimes that means coming back from the devastation of defeat, as we experienced in the Super Bowl."

EVERYTHING ON THE LINE

A desperate fourth-and-goal situation can make or break a game—or a career. Ask former Carolina Panthers quarterback Steve Beuerlein. He finished the 1999 season as the No. 2-rated quarterback in the NFL, second only to Super Bowl winner Kurt Warner. He passed for a league-high 4,436 yards (exceeding Warner's 4,353 yards), completing 343 of 571, with 36 touchdowns—a record that took him to his first Pro Bowl after thirteen years in the NFL. But all of that once hinged on a single fourth-and-goal play.

December 12, 1999, was bitterly cold in Green Bay, Wisconsin. The Carolina Panthers had battled the Green Bay Packers through four long, freezing quarters. With just five seconds remaining, Steve Beuerlein and the Panthers were on the Green Bay 5-yard line, trailing 31-27. A field goal wouldn't do—it was a touchdown or nothing.

And it was fourth and goal.

Beuerlein's job as starting quarterback was on the line. If he failed to produce on this one play, Carolina head coach George Seifert planned to start backup Jeff Lewis in next week's game. At thirty-four, Beuerlein had spent most of his career as a backup. His prior stints with the Raiders, Cowboys, Cardinals, and Jaguars had not been kind to

Beuerlein's body. Sacked 120 times in his career, he had undergone numerous surgeries and had a lot of bone chips and loose cartilage in his joints to show for it.

And now he needed all of his strength. If Carolina scored, the team would have a shot at a wildcard berth. If not, the Panthers' post-season hopes would die for another year—and Beuerlein's hopes to make a name in the NFL would die for good.

Steve Beuerlein

Beuerlein received the snap and took a short drop. He pump-faked. When the Packers' defense bit on the fake, Beuerlein tucked the ball and took off to the left side. Green Bay safety Rodney Artmore moved to cut him off, hitting Beuerlein low at the 2-yard line. It was a punishing, bone-rattling hit, but Beuerlein surged forward. As time expired, he extended himself across the goal line and his shoulders slammed into the end zone. But the pain didn't matter to Steve Beuerlein. From the ground, he threw his arms up and signaled: *Touchdown!*

The Panthers had won. And so had Steve Beuerlein.

The hardened steel within his soul was revealed in those five critical seconds, in those five desperate yards—

At fourth and goal.

A SIGN OF VICTORY

We all face fourth-and-goal situations in our lives. They arise at the office, in the home, and wherever we live our lives. A fourth-and-goal situation is a time of testing and pressure, when the clock is ticking, when an urgent decision must be made, when there are no second chances and a single mistake means disaster.

What if you blow it? What if you turn the ball over?

Fact is, a fumbled opportunity can often be just as valuable as a big win. It all depends on how you respond to it, what you learn from it, how you battle back from it. If you lose one game, there's always another game, another opponent, another fourth-and-goal opportunity to show the world what you're made of.

Sure, the opponents will only get tougher as you go. The crowd will get louder. The stakes will be higher, the risks greater. But when you win, the victory will be all the sweeter. You'll line up just yards from the goal line. As the clock ticks down, you'll take the snap, roll out, spin, break a tackle, extend the ball across the line—

Then, as a cheer shakes the air like a clap of thunder, you'll raise your arms in a sign of victory—

At fourth and goal.

After one fourth-and-goal play . . .
THE GAME WOULD NEVER BE THE SAME

The game of football was forever changed by one fourth-and-goal play. On December 18, 1932—thirty-four years before the first Super Bowl—what is now considered the first NFL championship game was played in Chicago. In times past, the league title was simply awarded to the team with the best record. But in 1932, two teams were tied for first place: the Chicago Bears, coached by the legendary George Halas, and the Spartans of Portsmouth, Ohio (who later became the Detroit Lions).

Red Grange

The game was originally scheduled for Wrigley Field until a storm dumped a foot of snow on the field. It then was moved to Chicago Stadium, an indoor hockey arena that had hosted a circus the previous day. The scent of elephant manure still perfumed the place. Fresh sod was laid between the hockey walls, creating a field that was only 60 yards long by 40 yards wide. The sidelines butted up against the stands.

Bronco Nagurski

The Collegiate Rulebook, the only rulebook used in the NFL at the time, required that a player be at least five yards behind the line of scrimmage before throwing a forward pass, but a fourth-and-goal play in the fourth quarter was about to change that rule. The game was scoreless, and the Bears had the ball on the Spartans' 2. It seemed an ideal moment to kick a field goal, but coach Halas called for a touchdown play instead. The ball was snapped to Carl Brumbaugh, who lateraled to running back Bronco Nagurski. Nagurski ran, then stopped before the line of scrimmage and zipped a pass to halfback Red Grange in the end zone. Touchdown!

Over Spartan objections, officials ruled the pass legal. A few plays later, the Bears padded their lead with a safety. At the final gun, the Spartans were shut out, 9-0—and the game of football was changed for good.

CHAPTER TWO

Trench Warfare

"He trains my hands for battle; my arms can bend a bow of bronze."

PSALM 18:34, NIV

Football is warfare.
So is life. And no
warfare is more
intense than
spiritual warfare.

Carolina Panthers defensive tackle Sean Gilbert has cussed out a lot of offensive linemen in his time. Early in his career, he played football not as a game of healthy aggression but as an act of violence.

During a 1993 game against the Arizona Cardinals, Gilbert (then with the L.A. Rams) got tangled near the bottom of a pile with then-Cardinals quarterback Steve Beuerlein. Gilbert put his hand under Beuerlein's face mask, grabbed Beuerlein's windpipe, and *squeezed*. When the officials got the pile untangled, Beuerlein jumped to his feet and took a few swings at Gilbert. "I thought I was going to die," Beuerlein said later.

But that was the *old* Sean Gilbert. Today there's a *new* Sean Gilbert—still playing hardcore, smash-mouth football, still one of the most aggressive players in the game. But the old trash-talking and foulness are gone. And he would never dream of choking an opposing player now.

The difference between the old Sean Gilbert and the new came in 1994. After achieving notoriety in the NFL, Gilbert realized that money and fame didn't satisfy. Neither did all the hedonistic pleasure his money could buy. He realized he was an empty man, living an aimless existence—and out of that emptiness, he made a decision to turn his life over to Jesus Christ.

"On October 12, 1994," he recalls, "I was born again. And when I got saved, my whole desire for everything in life, including this sport, changed. My focus is mainly on God right now, and I will hide this from no man. Because I do not play the game for any man. I play for God."

Just a few days before his conversion, Gilbert suffered a painful shoulder injury in a game against the Packers that left him sidelined till the following month. Even after his return, the injury hindered his playing ability. "I went to raise my arms sometimes, and I couldn't," he recalled.

Few people were aware of Gilbert's pain—so some blamed his impaired performance on his Christian faith. His newfound faith, they said, had made him "soft."

Gilbert's reaction? "That's just a lie," he says. "Man, we're playing football. You still try to bend a guy over backward. We don't have time to sit out there, trying to quote scriptures to guys all day. You're trying to execute the play."

Though Sean Gilbert's play suffered during the 1994 season, he came back the following year as physical as ever. In fact, Gilbert was so dominant that in 1998 the Carolina Panthers gave up two first-round draft picks and offered him a $46.5 million seven-year contract—at that time, the largest sum ever paid to a defensive player.

Sean Gilbert

THE BATTLEFIELD

Without question, football is a game of hard hits, intimidation, and emotional intensity. But is football a *violent* game? Former Detroit linebacker Reggie Brown can testify that this game certainly can have a violent impact on a human body. On Sunday, December 21, 1997, the Detroit Lions were leading the New York Jets 13-10 in the season-ender. The winner would go to the playoffs, and the loser would watch the playoffs on TV.

Early in the fourth quarter, Detroit's Barry Sanders ran for a touchdown, and the crowd shouted the lid off the Detroit Silverdome. After returning the kickoff, the Jets had trouble moving the ball. Quarterback Neil O'Donnell could scarcely call signals over the roar of 80,000 Motor City fans. On third down, O'Donnell handed off to

Neil O'Donnell

Adrian Murrell, who followed Lamont Burns on a draw play. Burns was hit by Detroit nose tackle Luther Elliss and driven back into Reggie Brown, who was coming across the line like a torpedo. The impact jammed Brown's spine with incredible force.

As the play was whistled dead, Brown lay flat on his back, unmoving. Ellis reached out a hand to help Brown to his feet, but Brown didn't respond. A horrific realization rippled through the Lions' defense: *Reggie's not getting up!* Several players screamed to the sidelines for help. Detroit's head trainer, Kent Falb, and team physician, Terry Lock, dashed to Brown's side. He was slipping into unconsciousness and had stopped breathing.

Working gently but quickly, they pried the helmet from Brown's head. Then Dr. Lock gave Brown mouth-to-mouth resuscitation.

Players from both teams shouted encouragement as an ambulance rolled onto the field. The Silverdome, which moments earlier had thundered with cheers, was deafeningly quiet. It took fifteen minutes to get Brown stabilized and attached to a ventilator.

As the ambulance left the field, Lions coach Bobby Ross gathered his team. "Listen," he said, "the league says we've got to finish this game. We've got to be professionals. There are two things we can do for Reggie right now. We can *pray* for him—and *play* for him." The chaplain led the players in prayer—prayer for Reggie Brown, and prayer for strength to finish the game.

As play continued, Brown was taken to the Pontiac Osteopathic Medical Center, where he battled for his life. A CAT Scan showed a serious contusion to his cervical spine but no fracture. Surgeons used a small piece of hipbone and titanium screws to fuse the bones at the top of his cervical spine. It was a winning day—for both the Lions and Reggie Brown. Today, he thanks God that he can walk. Even though the injury ended his NFL career, he was able to return to Texas A&M to pursue a degree in economics.

Reggie Brown credits the team trainer and doctor for saving his life. He also credits the prayers of the players

"Jesus called us to be meek, and meek means 'controlled aggression.' As a football player, that's one quality you definitely need. . . . Jesus went in the temple and overthrew the tables and said, 'Get out of my father's house! This is supposed to be a house of prayer!' I'm sure He wasn't smiling when He was doing these things. To do the things that Jesus did, He had to be aggressive."

MICHAEL BARROW
Linebacker, Carolina Panthers

and fans—and a miracle from God. So does quarterback Frank Reich, who was Brown's teammate at the time. Reich explained that their battle was waged not only on the gridiron, in the warfare of football, but also in the spiritual hearts of men—"but if you want to read about warfare, you can read all about it in the Bible."

BE A WARRIOR

It's true—football *is* warfare. So is life. Sometimes the drama of football merges with the drama of life. It might be Reggie Brown's dramatic struggle of life against death. Or it might be the dramatic struggle of love against hate, of good against evil. You can ask another Reggie about that struggle.

In January 1996, Reggie White and the Green Bay Packers were in San Francisco for the divisional playoff game. On the night before the game, the phone rang at the hotel desk. An anonymous caller said, "Reggie White's church is going to burn down. Tell him." Then the caller hung up. The hotel reported the call to the Packers' security chief, but because of the many crackpot calls the team had received that night, he thought it was a hoax. He decided not to tell Reggie.

The following morning, Reggie White and the Packers went out to Candlestick Park and beat the 49ers, 27-17. The victory over the defending Super Bowl champions was one of the most exciting wins of Reggie's career. But the exhilaration was short-lived.

Two days later, Reggie picked up his voice mail. One message was from a Knoxville reporter, informing Reggie that his church, the Inner City Community Church in Knoxville, Tennessee, had been firebombed and destroyed. Racist graffiti was found among the charred rubble.

Days later, Reggie learned of the anonymous call to his hotel. He also learned that the Inner City Community Church was not the first to burn. Many other African-American churches had already been torched across the

Reggie White

South, but it took the burning of an NFL star's church to bring the issue to national attention.

"The devil tripped himself up by attacking our church," Reggie later said. "He had seen all the good stuff our church had done—lives changed, people raised out of poverty and sin—so he tried to mess with us. That was his mistake. All things work together for good to those who trust Jesus, to those who are called to carry out His purpose in the world. *All* things—even the burning of a church."

Napolean Kaufman

Many good things came out of that evil, hateful act. The Green Bay community rallied together and raised money to rebuild the Knoxville church. Church youth groups from around the country supplied volunteer labor. Business owners donated construction materials and money, while school-children donated pennies. Reggie and his wife, Sara, were moved to tears by a nationwide outpouring of love and sharing.

A few months after the destruction of his church, Reggie White published his autobiography, *In the Trenches.* In it, he wrote:

> Trench warfare is rugged and dirty, but wars are won in the trenches. And make no mistake: Life is warfare. . . . The enemy is hate and racism. The enemy is ignorance and injustice. The enemy

is the System. The enemy is the devil. I've taken my share of hits from the enemy. I've been wounded a time or two. I bet you have, too. In this kind of warfare, the bones of our spirits may get broken, but they will mend. . . .

A church is made of people, not bricks and stone. The building has burned down, but the people are still standing. The devil has come against us. He has wounded us. He has destroyed much of what we have built. But the war is not over. The devil has not won.

And the devil will not win.

In football or life, there are really only two kinds of people: warriors and spectators. Life is warfare, and we must not be spectators. We must be warriors against hate and racism, against violence and destruction, against suffering and ignorance, against poverty and injustice. So get in the game. Get in the trenches.

You're a warrior in the biggest game of all.

A GAME OF PHYSICS—AND METAPHYSICS

Coach Vince Lombardi of the Green Bay Packers used to begin training camp by holding up a football and announcing, "Gentlemen, this is a football." Did his players understand what a profound statement that was? Do you?

Vince Lombardi

A football is not a simple object. Though it is called a *ball,* it is not *ball*-shaped. Examine any other ball—baseball, basketball, golf ball, tennis ball, handball— and you will see it is shaped like a sphere. But a football is shaped like—well, like a football.

The unique shape of a football imparts a mystical dimension to the game—the element of surprise. When a football hits the ground, it behaves unexpectedly. It takes weird hops and backward bounces because it is pointed at the ends. No one can predict which "way the ball bounces." It obeys the whim of chaos, not the nice, neat laws of Newtonian physics.

Life is not like round-ball games. Like football, life takes strange and unpredictable bounces.

But football is more than mere physics. It is also rich in metaphysical truths that probe the relationships between mind and matter, soul and substance. It is not, as some claim, a game of mindless violence. A well-played game is a thing of marvelous grace: The arching, spiraling trajectory of a Dan Marino pass. The agile artistry of a Deion Sanders' interception. The balletic grace of Reggie White as he leaps over a cut-blocking lineman to sack the quarterback. A well-played game is an act of sublime creation, skillfully wrought and precisely executed—a profound metaphysical experience.

Football is also a metaphysical paradox of cooperation and competition. Some critics claim that football is only about competition, about winners and losers. Not true. There is a cooperative arrangement between opponents. Eleven men line up opposite eleven other men, intent on defeating each other—yet they also cooperate to improve one another. Competition sharpens a man. Proverbs 27:17 tells us that just as iron sharpens iron, so one man sharpens another. True competitors tell one another, "You will sharpen me, and I will sharpen you. In the process of trying to defeat each other, we will bring out the best in each other."

That's football. And that's life.

CHAPTER THREE
Taking the Hit

*"But the LORD is with me
as a mighty, awesome One.
Therefore my persecutors will
stumble, and will not prevail."*

JEREMIAH 20:11

Adversity on the field is one thing. But what if you face adversity off the field as well— from the coaches, the media, and booing fans?

If quarterback Trent Dilfer could pick the most depressing day of his NFL career, it would likely be Game 2 of the 1998 season. That's when Dilfer and the Tampa Bay Buccaneers were demolished by the Packers at Lambeau Field, 23-15. Dilfer took six sacks and fumbled the ball away on three of them.

Those three turnovers not only cost Trent Dilfer a football game, they also cost him the confidence of Coach Tony Dungy. After that game, Dungy reined Dilfer in, restraining his natural aggressiveness by imposing a tight ball-control philosophy. Dilfer acknowledged that it was possible for some quarterbacks to win games playing Dungy's way, but it was not a system Dilfer felt he could succeed in. He was being asked to play against his strengths and instincts.

In October 1999, after the Bucs eked out a 6-3 win over the Chicago Bears, Dungy benched Dilfer. The benching lasted only one game, then Dilfer returned for three more winning starts in which the Bucs averaged 330 yards total offense per game. But in late November, Dilfer's season was ended by a broken collarbone.

Tony Dungy decided not to extend Trent Dilfer's contract, and the twenty-seven-year-old quarterback was out of a job and became a free agent. He was the winningest QB in Tampa Bay history, ranking No. 2 after Vinny Testaverde on the Bucs' all-time passing list with 12,969 yards. He was the only QB to lead the Bucs to three consecutive non-losing seasons and two playoff berths. He was team MVP in 1997 and the only Bucs QB selected to a Pro Bowl.

Who is the quarterback Dilfer identifies with most? "Jim Plunkett," Dilfer answers readily. Plunkett—the Raiders QB from the early '80s? Now, there's a name you don't hear much anymore. Why Plunkett? Because, says Dilfer, Jim Plunkett "struggled early, never quit, and couldn't care less if he's mentioned on the list of all-time greats. All he did was win."

The Plunkett-Dilfer similarities are striking. Both started their careers amid high expectations—Plunkett, a

Heisman winner, was drafted No. 1 by the Patriots in 1971; Dilfer was taken No. 6 in the '94 draft. Both saw their careers flop. Plunkett was cut, first by the Patriots and then the 49ers; the Bucs demoted then released Dilfer. Plunkett would later recall, "My confidence was at an all-time low. But I knew if I got into the right system I could excel." Dilfer felt the same way. In 1978 Jim Plunkett was picked up by the Raiders and given a second chance—and he led the Raiders to championships in Super Bowl XV and XVIII. And Dilfer? Like Plunkett, Trent Dilfer was a castoff QB who was placed in a system where he could excel—and boy did he excel!

Tony Boselli

Signed to a one-year contract by the Baltimore Ravens, Dilfer began the 2000 season as backup to Tony Banks. But during October, when the Ravens went twenty-one consecutive quarters without a single touchdown, Coach Brian Billick gave Dilfer the starting nod. Though Dilfer was not very productive in his first Ravens start— a 9-6 loss to Pittsburgh—he went on to win every other game that season *and* the post-season. That's *eleven* straight wins, including Super Bowl XXXV in Tampa Bay.

Some say Trent Dilfer only got his Super Bowl ring on the coattails of the Ravens' defense, which was arguably the best defensive unit in NFL history. But his contribution to the Ravens' championship season has been seriously underrated. As Ravens right guard Mike Flynn observed, "Trent sets a great tempo for our offense. When things go badly, he doesn't get rattled."

Case in point: The AFC Championship game, January 14, 2001, at Oakland's Network Associates Coliseum (a.k.a. "The Black Hole"). The game was scoreless early in the second quarter when Trent Dilfer took an 8-yard sack and found himself buried on his own 4. Instantly, 60,000 Raiders fans were on their feet, roaring for blood. But as he got up from the grass, he was actually *grinning*. Huddled in his own end zone, Dilfer calmly told his teammates, "Keep up the tempo and we'll draw them in. When they blitz, we'll burn 'em." Then he turned to tight end Shannon Sharpe and added, "I'm just waiting for the right matchup. Don't worry, it's coming to you."

On second and 18, Dilfer handed off to Jamal Lewis, who took it up the middle and was stuffed at the line of scrimmage. Returning to the huddle, Dilfer called a slant play. He took the snap, dropped five steps, and stood his ground against a massive Raider blitz. Sure enough, he had drawn them in. He launched a rocket over the middle. The target, as promised, was Sharpe.

Starting from the right slot, Sharpe cut across the middle, beat strong safety Marquez Pope, and caught the ball at the 12. Tucking the ball,

Sharpe blew past deep safety Anthony Dorsett, then chugged toward the far (*really* far!) end of the field. At 96 yards, it was the longest TD reception in post-season history, and the first strike in a definitive 16-3 victory that sent the Ravens to their first Super Bowl appearance.

CASTOFF TO CONQUEROR

During the 2000 season Trent Dilfer went from castoff to conqueror in a single season—a truly epic story. He almost seemed foreordained to that championship moment, as if some invisible hand of destiny were guiding his steps from humiliation to Super Bowl glory. How do you explain it?

To understand Trent Dilfer, you have to see his career as a *spiritual quest*. It has been about refining himself as a man of God. It has been about sublimating ego, vanquishing pride, and building a sturdy core of character in his soul. Dilfer is probably the most humble and self-effacing player in the NFL. Paradoxically, he is also supremely confident. It is hard for people to understand what Dilfer means when he says, "I want my legacy to be that I was the quarterback of the team that won the Super Bowl in spite of its quarterback." He has a clear-eyed view of himself, his abilities, and his limitations.

"Am I the most talented guy in the NFL? I don't believe so," Dilfer explains. "Am I the least talented? No, I don't think so. I do the best I can, I prepare very hard, and when I play, I leave everything out there. I try to be able to look my teammates in the eyes at the end of the game and tell them I gave everything I had." When he goes into the game, he gives it all he's got and wins.

Trent Dilfer's spiritual quest can be traced to his sophomore year at Fresno State University, when he turned his life over to Jesus Christ. In the years that followed, Dilfer learned that there is a big difference between being a Christian and being a *spiritually mature* Christian. That lesson came at a painful price when he was benched by Coach Dungy, which ended a streak of 70 consecutive starts. "It crushed me," Dilfer recalled. "My greatest fear in football was losing that streak."

Trent Dilfer

Amazingly, Trent Dilfer is now *grateful* that he was benched. He believes it was God's way of breaking him, so that he could be rebuilt into a better player and a better Christian. The week he was demoted, he says, "was one of the greatest in my life, spiritually, emotionally, with [his wife, Cassandra], and in practice. It was a giant, giant burden lifted off me— a burden of fear because the streak was the last thing I was holding on to."

For Coach Dungy, Trent Dilfer has nothing but praise. Returning to Tampa Bay for Super Bowl XXXV, he said, "Tony Dungy has had as much of an influence in my getting here as anyone, and Brian Billick has completed the equation. . . . I like Tampa, and I was treated well here. I looked around the stadium and thanked God for the great memories I have here."

Dilfer's faith enables him to look back on hard times without bitterness or resentment. Trusting God enabled him to withstand the criticism that was heaped upon him during his waning seasons in Tampa Bay.

OVERCOMING CRITICISM

The scorn of critics is a common affliction—even among the most legendary players in the game. Reggie White has endured criticism throughout his career, especially during his closing days with the Philadelphia Eagles. He played eight seasons with the Eagles and would have been content to finish his career there. Not only were he and his wife, Sara, intensely involved in a ministry to the poor, but Reggie believed the Eagles could win championships.

By early 1993, however, Reggie concluded that Eagles owner Norm Braman was unwilling to put up the money

"My Bible says that if you're going to get in the race, you should get in it to win. The men of the Bible weren't weak and passive. They were strong people who stood up for what they believed in— and they were sometimes stoned and beaten for it."

WILLIAM WHITE
Former Safety
Detroit Lions

to keep top-rank talent in Philly. So he reluctantly announced his departure and launched a seven-city tour in search of a new home. "God," he said, "will tell me where to go." Reggie wanted a shot at the Super Bowl and a venue for inner-city ministry. At the last moment, a $17 million dollar offer was submitted by an unlikely contender:

Cris Carter

the Packers of tiny Green Bay, Wisconsin. Fans were stunned when Reggie agreed to wear Packers green and gold.

Norm Braman said that Reggie's motivation for signing with Green Bay was "the reason most human beings make decisions today: money. ... Reggie White did a super job of marketing himself, and the press fell for all that [stuff] about God."

Reggie was hurt. "I never understood why Mr. Braman felt he had to question my integrity," he said. "He had this idea that Christians aren't supposed to care about money. He never understood me or what I was trying to do with the money I earned from playing football. I needed money to do ministry."

Reggie was vindicated when the Packers won Super Bowl XXXI. "People can laugh all they want," he said. "God has the last laugh."

The Bible tells us to expect opposition for our faith. "Yes, and all who desire to live godly in Christ Jesus will suffer persecution" (2 Tim. 3:12). And Jesus said, "Blessed are those who are persecuted for righteousness' sake, for theirs is the kingdom of heaven. Blessed are you when they revile and persecute you, and say all kinds of evil against you falsely for My sake. Rejoice and be exceedingly glad, for great is your reward in heaven" (Matt. 5:10–12).

Do you have what it takes to enter that arena? Do you have what it takes to plant your feet in the pocket, to take your stand against the blitz, to get driven into the turf for a few yards and a first down? And then do you have what it takes to get up and do it all over again for a few more yards?

If you do, then you have the makings of a champion.

Compare and contrast. . .
A TALE OF TWO SUPER BOWLS

The St. Louis Rams and the Baltimore Ravens—could you possibly name two more opposite teams in the NFL? And could two back-to-back Super Bowls provide more contrasts than XXXIV and XXXV?

Quarterback Kurt Warner and the Rams stormed Super Bowl XXXIV with a dazzling aerial attack. Warner completed 24 of 45 for a Super Bowl record of 414 yards, outgunning even the legendary Joe Montana. It was an epic battle to the final second, ending with the Titans falling *just one yard short* of a game-tying touchdown. The most unforgettable image of the game: Titans receiver Kevin Dyson on his back as time expired, vainly trying to extend the ball across the goal line.

The Rams were not known for their D, but oh, what an O! Super Bowl XXXIV was the capper of a glorious season in which Kurt Warner rocketed the ball for 4,353 yards and led the NFL with 41 TD passes (in the history of the NFL, only Dan Marino has thrown more TD passes in a season). Under Warner, the Rams improved from 4-12 in 1998 to 13-3 in 1999.

In XXXV, Ravens QB Trent Dilfer kept the game on the ground, throwing a mere 12 of 25 for 153. For the Ravens, the best offense proved to be a stingy, smashmouth defense. The combined defensive mass of Tony Siragusa and Sam Adams (670 pounds of flesh, bone, and gristle) acted like a steamroller, grinding the Giants' offense into the turf. While Dilfer's performance wasn't as flashy as Warner's, he walked off the field as much a Super Bowl champion as Kurt Warner.

Despite these contrasts, a closer look at Warner and Dilfer reveal some uncanny parallels. Both endured long, tortuous journeys to the Super Bowl. Both were cut from one team, then hired as backups by another. Both began to play only after the starting QB was taken out. In the end, both Dilfer and Warner defied the odds and garnered Super Bowl rings. And they both then stepped into the winner's circle to give honor to Jesus Christ.

Kurt Warner considers himself an ambassador for the Christian gospel. "It's not just stepping on a football field," he says, "but it's how it affects people's lives for Jesus. I think that's what helps me stay grounded—that I know I'm here to do the Lord's work."

Trent Dilfer's statement after Super Bowl XXXV was much like Warner's. As the confetti swirled around him, Dilfer said, "Everybody has been saying how great this feels. But what feels better is waking up every single morning and thanking God that life can be difficult at times, knowing that if you face it, and if you let God develop character in you and you face adversity head on, that this is what comes out of the other end."

Warner and Dilfer: Two quarterbacks as different as night and day, but identical in their triumph over adversity and their commitment to Christ.

CHAPTER FOUR

Encroachment!

"Husbands, love your wives,
just as Christ also
loved the church and
gave Himself for her."

EPHESIANS 5:25

In both football and in life, encroachment is one of the most common penalties of all. Individually, those little five-yard encroachment calls don't seem like much. But they add up.

Middle linebacker Mike Singletary is a Hall of Famer, a 10-time Pro Bowl player, twice named NFL Defensive Player of the Year ('85 and '88), and NFL Man of the Year ('90). For twelve years, he anchored the Bears' famed "Super Bowl Shufflers" defense—a defense that allowed fewer than 11 points per game in 1985. Mike Singletary was one of the principal reasons the '85 Bears finished 15-1 in the regular season and demolished the Patriots, 46-10, in Super Bowl XX. The Bears held the Patriots to only 7 yards rushing, and Singletary recovered two fumbles. He retired after the 1992 season, having spent his entire career wearing the wishbone C of the Chicago Bears.

His trademark was his *stare*. When those eyes glared at you from across the ball, something inside you turned to quivering lime Jell-O. On the field, Mike Singletary was a menacing, rib-crushing grizzly bear. But off the field? Would you believe . . . a teddy bear?

To his wife, Mike Singletary is a loving husband who prizes his wife and family above everything else in his life. To his three children—

Mike Singletary

Matthew, Kristen, and Jill—Mike Singletary is Daddy, a gentle and devoted father who has always given them his love, his hugs, and his time, no matter how busy his schedule.

Intensity in everything, giving it everything you've got—that's the hallmark of Singletary's soul. "In family," he says, "it means being there, spending time, teaching, loving, understanding. I teach my children about everything. I teach them about life in general—that life isn't fair; that you have to work for everything you get. I teach them to love family—that family is extremely important. And number one, I teach them to love Jesus Christ."

Sounds like a prescription for an idyllic family, doesn't it? But Mike

Singletary's home life hasn't always been a slide on ice. He met his bride Kim at Baylor University, and they married in May 1984. Several months into their marriage, Mike became troubled with intense feelings of guilt and unease. During their engagement, Mike had been unfaithful to Kim. He felt God calling him to open up his life, dispel the lies, and be honest about the past. God was telling him that the secrets he carried inside him were an encroachment on his marriage. It was hurting their relationship—and Kim didn't even know what the source of the hurt was. All she knew was that something wasn't right.

There is not very much in this world that scares Mike Singletary. A 300-pound offensive lineman certainly doesn't scare him. But the thought of being honest with Kim was almost more than he could handle. "God," he objected, "those acts of unfaithfulness all happened before we got married. That's just between You and me— why does Kim have to know?"

But God wouldn't let go of his conscience. The guilt kept him awake at night. Mike says, "David describes it very well in Psalms when he talks about [a man] weeping in his bones. It's a terrible feeling when the Lord's dealing with you and you won't listen."

"I don't separate my career from how I live as a man, so I try to be as consistent as possible in every facet of my life. . . . I think there's been a lack of men's leadership in family units for years. There's a huge void. One thing I'm really working on now— and it doesn't come naturally to me— is to be a family spiritual leader."

JOHN OFFERDAHL
Former Middle Linebacker
Miami Dolphins

During a vacation in the Caribbean, Mike worked up his courage and told Kim everything. As he talked, her eyes filled with tears of hurt. "Initially, I felt sorry for him," Kim recalls. "I [had seen] for a couple of months that he wasn't sleeping. He wasn't relaxed ever, and I could see he was really struggling with something. By the time he got it out, it had been really painful for him. . . . I knew he was repentant and remorseful, and I concentrated my focus on him. But later it seemed he got better, and I got angry."

At first, Mike's revelation didn't make his marriage any better—in fact, it made things many times worse. There were weeks of pain and anger. Kim considered separating from Mike, and it took her a year and a half to begin trusting him again. So how did Mike rebuild the trust? Through an intense, unwavering commitment to Christ.

He explains it this way: "She knew beyond a shadow of a doubt that I had really given my life to Jesus Christ, and I was going to be a man of faith. I tell her to this day, 'Sweetheart, I want you to understand something: I'm not going to fail you if I don't fail God. My eyes are on Him, and I've got to do the things that are right in His eyes. If I can please Him, then I know I won't have a problem pleasing you.'"

SINGLETARY'S "THREE Cs OF MARRIAGE"

Today, Mike and Kim Singletary keep their marriage strong by focusing on what they call "The Three Cs of Marriage." First C: *Communication.* In an interview with *Sports Spectrum*, Mike said that communication is more than just talking to each other. It is also compromising, helping, and being available to each other. "Bottom line," he says, "you have to be a servant."

Second C: *Commitment.* You have to take your wedding vows seriously, as a binding contract before God. All too often, people treat those words "as long as we both shall live" to mean "as long as I have warm fuzzy feelings." Romantic, passionate feelings come and go. But only a rock-solid, determined, promise-keeping *commitment* will carry a man and a woman through the tough times, the rocky times.

Third C: *Companionship.* A relationship involves work, but it should also be fun. There should be laughter and good times. Married couples shouldn't get so caught up in the routine of life that they forget to renew their friendship from day to day.

Frank Reich

Though Mike's honesty was painful for him and his wife, they ultimately have grown closer. "I can't believe how the Lord has used it," she says. "Mike finally arrived at where he was intended to be spiritually, where God wanted him to be as a man, as a leader, and as a public figure in this country. And I realized that my walk with God doesn't go through anybody else. It goes straight to the Lord."

KEEP UP YOUR GUARD

Mike Singletary is not alone. There are many players in the NFL who can testify about the pressures, distractions, and stresses that can encroach upon your most important priorities, including family.

"There are a lot of things that can come between you and your family," says Buccaneers coach Tony Dungy. "But family has to be the most important thing. And I think that's where your faith comes in. It keeps your priorities in line. It helps you remember that your family is much more important than your job."

Coaching an NFL team requires a huge commitment of time and energy, not only during football season but in the off-season as well. There are training camps and practices, personal appearances, media appearances, and community events. Tony Dungy makes it a priority to keep these work-related duties from encroaching on his family life. He plans dates with his wife, Lauren, and quality time with his family—bowling, swimming, or bike riding with his kids. It's not easy juggling his roles as husband, father, and coach of the Bucs, but Dungy meets that challenge on a daily basis.

"I hope [my kids] will see a consistent Christian," he says, "a husband who really puts Christ first, a dad who says, 'Follow my example—do what I do, not just what I say.' " Tony Dungy is a man who has decided never to let the demands of his career penalize his family.

Whether you make your living in a helmet and pads or a three-piece suit, never let your guard down against the things that would encroach on your relationship with God and with your family. If you keep up your guard, your family will never have to be penalized for your encroachment.

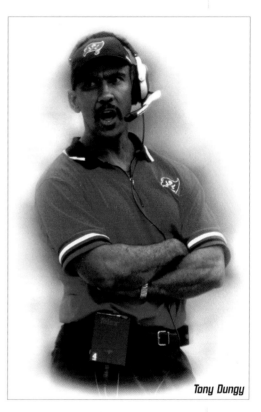

Tony Dungy

Singletary and his linebacker brethren . . .
GUYS WHO MAKE THE BIG HITS

In his book *Calling the Shots*, Mike Singletary described what it felt like to put a bone-shaking hit on an opponent: "The resultant feeling has always been almost indescribable to me, akin to being struck, I suppose, by a bolt of lightning—a blast that, for one brief second, shines through your mind and body like a flash of brilliant white heat." And Steelers Pro Bowl linebacker Greg Lloyd described what he felt after crashing full-tilt into Browns running back Kevin Mack: "I was dizzy, my head was hurting, and my eyes were watering. It felt good."

The heaviest hitters of the NFL are usually found (like Singletary) at the middle linebacker position. As the quarterback of the defense, the middle linebacker needs a rare combination of talents: intelligence (for reading offensive sets and calling defensive formations), cunning (for anticipating plays and eluding blockers), and raw, brute force. He throws his body around with total abandon, leaving a trail of busted helmets and tattooed opponents in his wake.

Just watch vintage film of Singletary in action. Look at the stormy glower of his eyes. Listen to him call across the line, "Come on! I'm waitin' for you, man! Come and get it!" That's intensity. That's power straining to be unleashed. During his four years at Baylor, he went through football helmets like some people go through Kleenex. The official count of busted helmets: sixteen.

Former quarterback Boomer Esiason said Singletary possessed a special quality: "sudden impact." Esiason explained, "Singletary could kind of float along the line of scrimmage. You couldn't find him, and then all of a sudden—*bam!*—there he was in the chest of the ball carrier. I mean, he's lifting him off the ground and pile-driving him."

The enforcers of the NFL take pride in their big hits. Jimmy Williams, a Sunday school teacher and former linebacker for the Lions, said, "I like to hit a man and hear that—that little moan." And Giants linebacker Lawrence Taylor sees pure poetry in that moment when "he doesn't see you coming and you drive your helmet into his back so hard he blows a little snot bubble."

And then there's The Tackle. It was November 20, 1960, the New York Giants versus the Philadelphia Eagles. The man who made The Tackle was the Eagles cement-contractor-turned-linebacker Chuck Bednarik. He drilled the Giants running back Frank Gifford in the chest, popped the ball free, and hammered the NFL's golden boy to the turf, where his head bounced a few times. The Eagles recovered and Bednarik was so happy, he danced around Gifford, shouting, "This game is over!"

But Gifford didn't move—he was out cold. First the crowd went silent. Then Bednarik went silent—he thought he had killed Gifford! Fact is, Gifford had a serious concussion that not only finished his season but also kept him out the entire *following* season.

Linebackers are the heart of fury in a ferocious sport. Remember the NFL slogan, "Feel the Power"? Linebackers put the *pow!* in power!

CHAPTER FIVE
Here Comes the Blitz

"Pray that you may not enter into temptation."

LUKE 22:40

Fame. Money. Time away from family. NFL players face more enticements in a single road trip than most of us face in a lifetime. How do they guard against the blitz of temptation?

The Saturday morning before Super Bowl XXXIII, Atlanta Falcons free safety Eugene Robinson was presented with the Bart Starr Award for high moral character. Nicknamed "Prophet," Robinson was widely known for his strong Christian witness. That evening, Eugene Robinson was arrested for soliciting a Miami undercover police officer dressed as a prostitute.

The media quickly piled on the criticism. "This is why we do not listen," wrote one columnist. "This is why we do not trust what we hear. This is why we often do not write all that athletes say. Because of mornings like this." Another grumbled, "I'm not only up to my neck in testosterone-laden, self-indulgent players, I'm God-squadded out by the hipper hypocrites and pseudomoralists of the bunch."

Is Eugene Robinson a hypocrite? No. He's a man who believes in Jesus and tries to follow his Lord. But he is also a man who is all too aware of his own feet of clay, his own inner struggle against temptation and sin. No Christian is immune from that struggle. Only a year earlier, Robinson told *Sports Spectrum* magazine:

> Right at the end of Romans 7, it explains how your faith affects your life. There's this constant battle that goes on, a war within you. You need to recognize that and then recognize the dependence you have to have on God.
>
> Human philosophy would tell you that there's good in every man. But the Bible says, "There is no one righteous, not even one!" (Romans 3:10). It also says, "The heart is deceitful above all things and beyond cure. Who can understand it?" (Jeremiah 17:9). That speaks to the heart of man that God knows. He knows you.
>
> When you quiet your heart and you're all alone and given the opportunity to do wrong, the Bible says you'll opt for that opportunity if you're not controlled by the Holy Spirit.

These are the words of a man who fully understood the war within and the deceptiveness of the human heart. Tragically, Eugene Robinson momentarily forgot his own advice. He took a little time off from his dependency upon Christ—and there was a price to pay.

After his arrest and release, Robinson returned to his hotel but didn't sleep that night. The distraction and sleeplessness appeared to hurt his performance in the Super Bowl. In the second quarter, Denver's receiver Rod Smith burned Robinson with a post move to the middle and breezed into the end zone. That play took the starch out of the Falcons' defense and became the turning point in the game.

Eugene Robinson

If Eugene Robinson had not lost the struggle against temptation, if he had possessed just an ounce more focus and energy at that key moment, could it have changed the entire tenor of the game? We will never know . . . and neither will Eugene Robinson.

After the game, Robinson appeared before reporters and said, "I apologize to my Lord, Jesus Christ, my wife and kids, and the tremendous NFL family for the distraction this has caused. . . . I had lots of time last night to think about how I was going to respond. The ramifications are far-reaching. Confession is good for the soul, but bad for the reputation. I truly love my wife and kids, and I regret that this has hurt them." He later returned the Bart Starr Award.

Eugene Robinson is not a prophet, not a plaster saint. He's a man who has wrestled with man-sized temptations. He's no different from the rest of us. We all have a war raging within us. We all face attack from our enemy, and this enemy knows our vulnerable points. He will destroy us if he can.

We cannot condemn Eugene Robinson. But we can learn the lesson of his personal failure.

WHEN THE BLITZ COMES

Your soul is under assault. The blitz is coming. If you are not ready for it, it will roll right over you. So dig in and stand firm. Let these battle-seasoned men of the NFL tell you how.

Offensive tackle Anthony Muñoz went into USC a confirmed, hard-drinking party animal. But midway through his college career, he realized that his life was empty. So he left his former life and turned his life over to Jesus Christ. Sometimes he slipped back into the old ways, but each time he returned to the Lord with a renewed determination to resist temptation and follow his Lord.

As he matured in his faith, Anthony Muñoz developed what he calls a "Stay Safe" approach that has served him well amid the massive temptations that came his way as a player with the Cincinnati Bengals. The "Stay Safe" method is based on two passages of Scripture:

> "Flee sexual immorality. Every sin that a man does is outside the body, but he who commits sexual immorality sins against his own body." 1 Corinthians 6:18

"Flee also youthful lusts; but pursue right-eousness, faith, love, peace with those who call on the Lord out of a pure heart."
2 Timothy 2:22

Flee? Since when does a Hall of Fame offensive tackle need to flee from anything? But Muñoz knows there are some things too big for *any* guy to handle. Temptation is one of them. "The Lord tells us to flee," he says. "It's a command. We're smart enough to know when we're going to be in a situation that will be a temptation. You've just got to say 'adios' and leave."

As an offensive lineman, Anthony Muñoz knows what a blitz is all about. He's had a lot of experience blocking out defenders who are trying to get to his quarterback. And he knows that the most dangerous blitz of all is the blitz of temptation. "You can allow the temptations and the things that go along with this game to sidetrack you and take you off the road of walking with the Lord," he says. "You name 'em, they're there. Notoriety, wealth, materialism."

Anytime temptation might be an issue, Muñoz practices his "Stay Safe" approach and flees the situation. He also practices these key principles to keep himself safe:

"There's a whole lot more to being abstinent than not having sex. It's a lifestyle. I've got a couple of Christian friends who hold me accountable for my actions."

JUSTIN ARMOUR
Former Wide Receiver
Denver Broncos

1. *Be careful what you take into your mind and soul.* Muñoz is very selective about what he feeds his mind through television, movies, music, books, magazines, and the Internet. If you pollute your mind with moral garbage, what kind of moral output do you expect to produce?

Anthony Muñoz

2. *Fill your mind with positive, uplifting truth.* If you don't fill your free time with positive things, you open yourself to temptation. Muñoz makes a point of reading his Bible and other Christian books, especially when traveling or relaxing.

3. *Spend time in prayer.* For Muñoz, that means spending time alone with God, and spending time praying with his wife, DeDe, and their children, Michael and Michelle.

Another defense against temptation is practiced by linebacker Peter Boulware of the Baltimore Ravens. Boulware relies on maintaining accountability relationships with other Christian men. During his days at Florida State, he found another player, defensive end Andre Wadsworth, who shared his Christian values. They prayed and studied the Bible together and held each other accountable for a godly lifestyle.

"We refrained from going out drinking at clubs," Boulware says, "and from having sex and things like that. There are a lot of people pulling at you to do the wrong things. And it's tough by yourself when you're trying to live right and to do the right thing. But Andre and I would encourage each other and keep each other accountable.

"Now that I'm in the NFL," he reflects, "I still find it essential to have other Christians who encourage and challenge me the same way Andre did when we were in college. I choose my closest friends by looking at the way they're living. . . . These types of friendships help me stand strong against the harmful temptations that often accompany my life in the NFL."

TAKE YOUR STAND

Dr. Bruce Wilkinson, founder of Walk Thru the Bible Ministries and a frequent speaker with Promise Keepers, suggests a simple but powerful prayer he calls the "Three-Minute Temptation Buster." In *Experiencing Spiritual Breakthroughs*, he says he noticed that his own times of greatest temptation always came at times of emotional distress. So he asked God to show him another way to find comfort from distress other than yielding to temptation. Then it came to him: Wasn't the Holy Spirit also called "The Comforter"? What would happen, Wilkinson wondered, if he specifically asked for comfort in times of temptation? So he decided to pray for God's comfort.

"I feel good that I have taken care of myself. The Bible says we should treat our bodies like a temple and that's what I try to do. I don't see the point of [using drugs] at all."

ROBBIE TOBECK
Center, Atlanta Falcons and
Seattle Seahawks

My simple request went like this: "Dear Holy Spirit, You've been sent to me to be my personal Comforter. I am in desperate need of comfort. I don't want to sin. Please comfort me. In Jesus' name, Amen."

That was it. I took off my watch to see what would happen and when. At first, absolutely nothing did. . . . But then I slowly became aware of something—I felt comforted! . . . My soul felt soothed and no longer in pain.

When I turned back toward that temptation, I discovered it had miraculously slithered into the darkness, far away from my senses. I was free.

Wilkinson adds that he has prayed that prayer many times since, and he has checked his watch to time the Holy Spirit's response. Every time—without exception!—the Comforter has responded in three minutes or less. The next time you are tempted, try Bruce Wilkinson's "Three-Minute Temptation Buster" and see if God doesn't come through for you.

YOU CAN LINE UP AND PLAY AGAIN

Falling to temptation can bring enormous hurt, shame, and humiliation on yourself and the people who depend on you. But even if you have already fallen, you need to know that your life is not over, nor is your usefulness to God. There is hope and forgiveness available to you.

Dwight Stephenson, the Hall of Fame center for the Miami Dolphins (1980-87), put it this way: "The Bible says in Acts 3:19,

'Repent, then, and turn to God, so that your sins may be wiped out.' The great thing about life with Jesus is that it's like football—if you make a mistake, you can line up and play again. That doesn't mean you want to make mistakes; it means we have a forgiving God."

Defensive end John Burrough, now of the Minnesota Vikings, played for Atlanta during Super Bowl XXXIII. He was one of the Christian brothers who stood by Robinson after his fall on Super Bowl eve. "At first we couldn't believe it," Burrough recalls. "But when we found out it was true, every Christian I spoke with immediately prayed for Eugene and his family. . . . It was like the story in the Bible of David, a man who desired to have God's own heart and to make God's desires his own. David had been raised in stature by God, but he started to turn to his own fleshly existence, and God called him on it. When he fell, he was surrounded by other believers who helped bring him back up and refocused his faith on God. . . .

"Eugene Robinson is a strong Christian man who fell. He fell flat on his face, but I guarantee that he's a better Christian today because of what happened."

No matter who you are, no matter what you do, temptation is out there, gunning for you. Look out! Here comes the blitz! If you are ready for it, then even though others may stumble and fall, you'll be able to stand—

And *win.*

Frank Reich and the Bills make . . .
THE GREATEST COMEBACK OF ALL

Ever get so deep in the hole you felt like giving up before halftime? Quarterback Frank Reich and the Buffalo Bills knew that feeling.

In the AFC wild card game, played on January 3, 1993, it seemed as though the Bills' offense couldn't get going, and the Houston Oilers couldn't be stopped. By halftime, Oilers quarterback Warren Moon had drilled home four TD passes, amassing a huge 28-3 lead. Reich, subbing for injured Jim Kelly, couldn't get into a rhythm—and the Bills' defense seemed as porous as Swiss cheese.

In the locker room at halftime, the Bills' coaches yelled at the players and the players yelled at one another, all trying to convince one another they could still win this game and stay in the playoffs. Amid the shouting, third-string QB Gale Gilbert took Frank Reich aside. "Listen," Gilbert told Reich, "you did it before when you were in college. You can do it again today." Gilbert was talking about a 1984 game in which Reich had rallied his Maryland team from a 31-0 deficit to a 42-40 victory over Miami.

At the start of the second half, Reich prayed for a miracle and reached back to his memories of that college game, seeking inspiration. But only five plays into the half, disaster struck: Reich was intercepted. Houston strong safety Bubba McDowell snagged the ball and ran it 58 yards for a touchdown. The stunned Bills trailed by 32 points. No NFL team had ever come back from such a deficit.

Disgusted fans rose from their seats and filed out of the stands. Though deflated, Reich somehow found the strength to keep going. He mounted a courageous drive that ended with a one-yard TD run by Kenneth Davis. After that touchdown, the Bills recovered an onside kick, and Reich went back to work. In fact, he capped each of the Bills' next three possessions with touchdown passes. In all, the Bills scored four TDs in 6:52—the most productive third quarter in playoff history.

Meanwhile, the Bills' defense went to a basic 3-4 in the second half to stop Warren Moon's passing game. It worked. The Oilers' offensive production completely shut down, giving the Bills' offense a chance to catch up.

In the fourth quarter, with only 3:08 left, the Bills took a 38-35 lead with a 17-yard Reich-to-Andre Reed TD pass. The Oilers battled back, driving to within field goal range. With just 15 ticks left in regulation play, Al Del Greco kicked a 26-yarder to send the game into overtime.

Three plays into OT, Warren Moon overthrew Ernest Givins. Bills cornerback Nate Odomes was there for the interception. Result: a Steve Christie field goal to win the game. As Rich Cimini reported in *Newsday,* Frank Reich "took his greatest college game and replayed it in the NFL." It was a win for the record books—a game now known as The Comeback.

The moral to the story? Well, there are two: First, if you're a fan, never leave the stadium until it's really over, or you just might miss the game of the century. Second, no matter who you are, no matter how badly you've blown it, never give up hope. As long as there is time on the clock, you've got a game to play and a chance to win.

Just ask Frank Reich.

CHAPTER SIX

Go Deep!

"Confess your trespasses to one another, and pray for one another, that you may be healed. The effective, fervent prayer of a righteous man avails much."

JAMES 5:16

The Bible challenges us to "go deep" and "feel the power" of God. How about you? Are you content to merely skim the surface of life— or are you ready to go deep?

"It's the latest thing," observed one *Sports Illustrated* commentator. "Ringed by TV Minicams, a dozen or so fervent Christian players from both teams join at midfield after the game, drop to their knees, clasp hands, bow heads, and pray. A stadium full of people and a national television audience are in attendance, whether they like it or not."

The *SI* writer went on to quote tight end Howard Cross of the Giants. "It's a testimony," said Cross. "We want people to notice." Howard Cross is the man who organized the first post-game prayer huddles. It began in 1987, when Cross played for the University of Alabama and led the Crimson Tide's chapter of Fellowship of Christian Athletes. Cross and his Christian teammates agreed with players at Penn State to huddle after an upcoming game. The Alabama-Penn State prayer huddle created a few lines of mention in the media, then was forgotten.

But Howard Cross didn't forget. When he moved to the NFL, so did the prayer huddle idea. The first post-game prayer meeting in the NFL came after a Giants-49ers game at Candlestick Park, December 3, 1990.

Members from both teams, including Cross, knelt and thanked God for a well-played game. As they prayed, however, the TV cameras were focused on a post-game shouting match between Giants quarterback Phil Simms and 49ers cornerback Ronnie Lott.

Still, the practice continued and spread to other teams. In January 1991, after the Giants narrowly beat the Buffalo Bills, 20-19, in Super Bowl XXV, the victors and vanquished met on the field, embraced one another, and prayed together. It was that Super Bowl huddle that prompted the *Sports Illustrated* writer to grouse about the prayer phenomenon in the NFL.

"When we bow down," said Cross in *SI*, "we're showing them that we're looking for more than this world has to offer. Some people think it's weak, but some people say, 'Boy, I'm really touched by that.' And if we touch one person, then it's worth it."

"Personally," the *SI* commentator scoffed, "I think it's weak. I don't think your average fan goes to football games to be touched. I don't think that when he loads up the thermos and pays $10 to park, he's looking to get proselytized. The only conversions he cares about are extra points. Sure, athletes are entitled to freedom of religion like anybody else. But let them exercise it on their own time. . . . I hope that the NFL will have the good sense to curtail these huddles."

That commentary appeared in February 1991. A few months later, the league issued a rule prohibiting players from lingering on the field after games. Eagles defensive end Reggie White believed the rule was aimed at halting prayer huddles. "I think there are people running the league," Reggie observed, "who are embarrassed by the fact that Christian football players pray together. Whatever the league's reasons for that rule, Keith Byars, Keith Jackson, and a lot of players chose to openly defy it because it was wrong, it was discriminatory, and we couldn't abide by it. The league backed down."

What do players pray about? Do they enlist God's help in winning the game? "Of course not," answers Reggie White. "We don't ask God for victory on the field. We just ask Him to help us play a good, clean game, and

"Read, study, learn, that's all I do, because it's a high calling. Before I found Christ, I had all the material comforts and all the money and all the fame and popularity, but I had no peace. When I found Christ, I found what I had been missing all those years."

DEION SANDERS
Cornerback & Wide Receiver
Dallas Cowboys,
Washington Redskins

that He will protect the players of both sides. We finish by saying the Lord's Prayer together."

In a prayer huddle, one player may thank God that players on both sides came through the game without severe injury. Another may ask that any who are injured would recover quickly. Another may ask that the visiting team have a safe trip home to their families. That's it. That's what the *SI* writer found so threatening.

Critics don't seem to understand the close connection between football and faith. Football is an emotionally and physically intense game. At the end of each game, there is a winner—and there is a loser. Winners need the discipline of prayer to keep them humble and focused so that they can continue to play hard week after week. Losers need the encouragement of prayer. Through prayer, they can find the hope that today's loss can be put in the past, and next week's game will tell a different story.

When teammates pray, relationships are forged and the souls of warriors are bonded together. The best coaches in the game—whether believers or not—welcome prayer in the locker room and on the field. When Reggie White played for coach Buddy Ryan in Philadelphia, Ryan told him that he wanted Christian athletes on his team. Why? Because Christians work for a higher calling than mere money, fame, and ego. "Coach Ryan told me," said White, "that Christians are some of the hardest workers he's been around, that most of the time they've got their priorities squared away and understand what it takes to be a champion."

Most important of all, when players pray together, it's not just an act or a show intended to impress. It's an extension of the daily reality of the players' lives. They pray in the morning, at mealtimes, and at night. They pray whenever they face a major challenge. They thank God whenever they surmount a major obstacle. Former Saints quarterback Danny Wuerffel says, "Folding my hands together following each touchdown is a humble way of thanking the Lord for the gifts and opportunities He has so graciously bestowed on me. Praying wasn't anything I planned or decided to do, but I found it to be as natural as spotting an open receiver and instinctively throwing the ball."

For some, prayer is part of the thrill of the game. After Cowboys defensive tackle Russell Maryland won his ring in Super Bowl XXVII, he reflected, "My greatest Super Bowl memory was the chapel service at the hotel just prior to the game. We all got in a circle and held hands and prayed. Some of the players thanked God for the opportunity to play in such a big game, and others thanked God for their parents. The feeling I got from that few moments of prayer was just incredible."

BEYOND THE SURFACE

Just as the NFL once tried to ban on-field prayer from pro football, the NCAA tried to ban prayer from collegiate football in 1995. Such harmless expressions as dropping to one knee or folding hands in the end zone were outlawed as "excessive celebration." After the NCAA was taken to court, the rules were relaxed.

Some will say, "Sure, athletes are entitled to freedom of religion, but let them exercise it on their own time." They seem to forget that when an athlete is on the field, that *is* his time. The First Amendment doesn't just guarantee us freedom of religion behind closed doors, but also in the end zone or in front of a TV camera.

Just as important as your right to practice your faith in public is the need to build your relationship with God within the confines of your soul. Ultimately, that's what it really means to "go deep" with God. Tight end Ernie Conwell of the Rams puts it this way: "One of the things God has been teaching me is that I need to continually ask for wisdom and understanding. To go deeper into my walk with Him. . . . Seeking God in prayer, reading the Word, spending time with believers, having other believers in my life who can disciple me and mentor me."

Just as great coaching makes great football players, great Christian mentoring builds strong believers. Only when you surround yourself with people of faith and spiritual maturity can you truly "go deep" into faith and spiritual maturity. This is what guard Adam Timmerman found when he began his NFL career in Green Bay. Timmerman and his wife, Jana, believe it was God's plan for him to be drafted by the Packers, where he came under the mentoring of the team's spiritual leader, Reggie White.

"I really wasn't totally living the way I should be," Timmerman recalls, "and after coming to the Packers, I met some good role models. I think that's when the big change occurred in my life. I had asked the Lord to take over my life before, and I wasn't sure what that totally meant. I think I've become a more spiritual man now."

Green Bay is where another mentoring friendship was formed between offensive tackles John Michels and Ken Ruettgers. "As I've grown in my relationship with [Jesus Christ]," says Michels, "I've learned that God loves me unconditionally. This is the type of friendship He desires for me to have with others. Instead of friends who like me because I'm an NFL player, I look for friends who like to be around me because of who I am as a person.

Adam Timmerman

"This is the type of friendship I've formed with Ken Ruettgers. Ken played with the Packers for twelve years and is the player I was drafted to replace when he was nearing retirement. He is ten years my senior, but we both learn a great deal from each other. . . . Ken has helped me mature more and more into the type of man I want to be."

Joe Gibbs was head coach of the Washington Redskins for twelve years before his retirement in 1993. He coached his team to four Super Bowls, including three wins, and was inducted into the Pro Football Hall of Fame in 1996. The year after his third Super Bowl win, his Winston Cup racer, with Dale Jarrett at the wheel, won the Daytona 500. Known for his unrelenting work ethic, Gibbs has been a business-man, coach, race team owner, broadcaster, husband, and father. But above all else, Joe Gibbs is a Christian who goes deep into his faith through prayer, Bible study, and Christian relationships. These spiritual disciplines help him balance all aspects of his hard-charging, high-octane life.

"I have a lot of things I like to do," he reflects. "I'm competitive and have a tendency to be involved in big things that take me away from home. I'm trying to build race teams and a business. Back when I was trying to build a football team, my biggest concerns were always, 'What do I do with my time? How much do I spend in ministry? How much do I spend with my family, and how much do I spend in my job?'

"I think for a lot of us that's one of the biggest challenges in life. I think the right answer is to ask Him to guide us through all the decisions we make. The way to do that is to be in prayer and Bible study—daily, continuously. That way God can move in your life. If you seek Him and ask Him to lead you as to where you should spend your time, then He's going to lead you. Constant communication with the Lord is key."

Pro Bowl defensive tackle Luther Elliss of the Detroit Lions puts it this way: "The hunger I have now is for Christ. I'm hungry to know who He is. I want to know the Bible from Genesis to Revelation. I want to know the historical side and the background of the Bible. I want to know what the culture was like at that time. I want to know what God has in store for me. I just have this hunger to know."

So take a lesson from the greats of the NFL. "Feel the power" of prayer. "Go deep" with God by studying His Word. You want intensity in your life? Then build intense relationships with other believers,

Joe Gibbs

and make sure you have some intense mentoring and coaching relationships with people who will challenge you to do your utmost for God's highest calling.

Don't be content to just skim the surface of life. Go deep!

Praise the Lord and pass the football...

THE FAITH AND FOOTBALL CONNECTION

Faith and football. Seems as though they've always belonged together.

The connection probably goes back to Notre Dame University, where so many football traditions began. Notre Dame is where quarterback Gus Dorais and split end Knute Rockne came up with a nifty innovation called the "forward pass" and transformed the game in 1913. Rockne later coached at Notre Dame. There, in 1920, he called in a priest to pray for halfback George Gipp, who lay dying of pneumonia. Before the Gipper passed on, he told his coach, "Someday, Rock, when the odds are against us, ask the team to win one for the Gipper. . . . I'll know about it and I'll be happy." A football player died, but a football legend was born.

Long before controversies over post-game prayer huddles, prayer was an integral part of Notre Dame football. Every Notre Dame player attended a pre-game mass, said the Lord's Prayer together, and took communion together.

And even today, if you visit the Notre Dame campus, one of the great symbols of the school's faith-and-football heritage towers over you—the fourteen-story mural on the south wall of Hesburgh Library, called "Touchdown Jesus." It is a truly amazing image of Jesus with his arms raised as if to signal—*Touchdown!* The football symbolism was unintended by the artist, but was it unintentional on God's part? Is it purely coincidental that "Touchdown Jesus" is clearly visible over the north end zone of the football stadium?

At another institution of higher learning, a well-known legend of faith and football began. On September 28, 1963, McMurry College of Abilene, Texas, played against Northeast Louisiana in Monroe. After the game, the McMurry Indians boarded an aging DC-3 for the flight home. When the pilots and flight attendants showed up late, they scrambled to prepare for takeoff. In his haste, the pilot neglected to remove the lock from the tail elevators. The plane took off, but had trouble climbing. Then during the attempted landing, the plane smashed onto the runway, damaging the landing gear, and bounced back into the air. The pilot announced that they would have to crash-land at a nearby airbase.

Touchdown Jesus Mural

The plane circled for four hours, burning off fuel. Inside the plane, the twenty-eight players and three coaches of the McMurry Indians contemplated the meaning of life—and eternity. During those dark hours, the players asked their coach to pray on their behalf. So he prayed. That coach was Grant Teaff, who later became the legendary coach of the Baylor Bears.

Finally, the plane descended toward the airbase in Shreveport and belly-landed with a scream of bare metal on tarmac. The plane skidded for a seeming eternity, then groaned to a stop. The players jumped out and surrounded Coach Teaff as he offered a prayer of thanks. "That experience," Teaff recalled, "changed my life. . . . I committed my life to God." He later had cards printed up proclaiming the McMurry players and coaches to be members of the "Brotherhood of Indian Belly-Landing Experts" (B.I.B.L.E.). Since then, Grant Teaff has been tireless in his Christian witness.

Deion Sanders

Faith and football also connected when the Hail Mary was born. That famous desperation throw into the end zone got its name from a playoff game between the Cowboys and Vikings on December 28, 1975. In the final minute of the game, Cowboys quarterback Roger Staubach lofted a 50-yard pass to Drew Pearson. As the saying goes, Staubach put up a prayer. The ball slipped through Pearson's hands, and he thought he had dropped it—then he found it trapped under his arm. He sped for the end zone for a touchdown—and an answered prayer.

In the locker room after the game, Staubach described his feelings as he threw that pass. "I closed my eyes," he said, "and said a Hail Mary"—and a desperation throw to the end zone has been called a Hail Mary ever since.

There is a saying in Dallas that the hole in the roof of Texas Stadium was put there so that God could watch the Cowboys play. Maybe so. But the shape of a football stadium should also suggest to us a deeper truth about the Christian life. Just as the players on a field are being watched from the stands by thousands of spectators, our lives as Christians are also under intense scrutiny. We are surrounded by people watching us, cheering for us, counting on us to win.

Hebrews 12:1 tells us, ". . . since we are surrounded by so great a cloud of witnesses, let us lay aside every weight, and the sin which so easily ensnares us, and let us run with endurance the race that is set before us, looking unto Jesus, the author and finisher of our faith."

CHAPTER SEVEN

Giving Back

*"I beseech you therefore, brethren,
by the mercies of God, that you
present your bodies a living
sacrifice, holy, acceptable to God,
which is your reasonable service."*

ROMANS 12:1

NFL stars play the most punishing team sport of all, but could it be that under all that physical aggression and emotional intensity, there beats not only a heart of gold, but the heart of God?

Two inner-city kids were arguing on a D.C. street corner. Approaching this scene was Washington Redskins cornerback Darrell Green. He had seen it all before: Trash-talk and smack-talk escalating to full-scale bloodletting. But just as Green was about to step in, one of the kids said, "Hey, man, I'm not fighting you. It's not worth anyone getting hurt."

Green realized that the young peacemaker was one of the kids who had been helped by the Darrell Green Youth Foundation. "It brought tears to my eyes," Green said as he related this story. "These kids were practicing what we've been preaching—loving one another and living the Kingdom way."

The Foundation began in 1994 at a housing project in Washington, D.C., taking thirty-three kids through a values training course. The young people, ages six through sixteen, signed a pledge to revere God, respect others, and resolve disagreements in a nonviolent way. The Foundation provided the kids with field trips, food, clothing, tutoring, and Bible-based learning. Green's goal is to change the direction of inner-city lives, to shield kids from the destructive influences of drugs, violence, and moral pollution—and to introduce them to Jesus Christ.

The Darrell Green Youth Foundation has spread to other parts of D.C. and beyond, and Green has poured hundreds of thousands of his own dollars into the program and has enlisted the involvement of businesses and private individuals. Why does he do it? Because he feels richly blessed by God—and he wants to *give back*.

Darrell Green has been called "the fastest man in the NFL." He's also been called "ageless" because of his eighteen seasons in the NFL. In May of 2000—at the ripe old age of forty, no less!—he signed a five-year contract extension with the Washington Redskins. After inking the new contract, he went out on the track and ran the 40-yard dash in a blazing 4.24 seconds.

But Darrell Green puts out his greatest energy on behalf of kids and the Lord Jesus. His message to anyone who will listen is to go and do likewise. "Hey, people!" he says. "Organize. Mount up. Bring your resources. Go into your communities. You can go one day a week and share the gospel. Help. Little, average, normal people, sitting in the pews, you who know the Bible backward and forward, take your gifts and talents and go down the street and organize in somebody's basement or garage. Even if it's just two or three kids, do what Matthew 28 says."

Giving back. That's a theme you hear from one NFL star after another. "My whole thing is giving back to the community," says tight end Keith Jackson, a Pro Bowl veteran of the Eagles, Dolphins, and Packers. "To whom much is given, much is required. I think God has blessed us [football players] with a lot of things, and it's time for us to start giving back." One of the ways Keith Jackson gives back is through PARK (Positive Atmosphere Reaches Kids), a $5.2 million Christian recreation and education project that he helped found in Little Rock, Arkansas, where he grew up.

Keith Jackson

Another way Keith gives back is by living up to his position as a Christian role model. "Every Christian should be a role model," he says, "because Jesus said, 'Let your light shine before men, that they may see your good deeds and praise your Father in heaven' (Matt. 5:16). . . . Once we accept Christ, we're all thrown into a position of being a role model—actually being an image of Christ."

Despite the bad press football players often get, studies show that they are statistically *better behaved* than the general population—especially when you factor in the deprived inner-city background of many players. Perhaps the reason football pros tend to be less criminally inclined than the general population is because they are better educated than the general population (they are almost all college graduates). Or perhaps it is because the NFL promotes good values for the sake of the league's image. Or it could be the result of so many players in the game who exemplify strong Christian values.

Cris Carter

USE YOUR PLATFORM

A term you often hear from Christian football players is *platform.* "I've been blessed with the opportunity to be on the field and have a platform," says linebacker Hardy Nickerson (Steelers, Bucs, Jaguars). "And I want to make sure that I use this platform—first, to glorify God and then to help people and be an encouragement to them."

Cris Carter agrees. "The NFL is a tremendous platform," he says.

"I would say halfway through my career I used that platform to promote myself. Somewhere along the way I switched and realized it wasn't about me. It was about other people." He spoke those words as he became the thirtieth recipient of the NFL's Man of the Year Award—and the first to win it since it was renamed in honor of Walter Payton. Carter received the award for the way he used his NFL platform to serve his community—by founding CAUSE (Christian Athletes for Spiritual Empowerment)—and for supporting inner-city schools, the Special Olympics, the Boy Scouts, and the Make-A-Wish Foundation. He donated the $25,000 Payton prize to CAUSE.

Cleveland Browns kicker Phil Dawson is another player who views his role in football as a platform for sharing his faith. Dawson gained attention during a game against the Cincinnati Bengals when he became one of the few placekickers to score a touchdown. It came in October 1999 as the 0-4 expansion Browns were playing at home in quest of their first win of the post-Art Modell era. The Bengals were leading 6-0 in the second quarter as the Browns drove to the Bengals 4-yard line. On fourth-and-goal, the Browns brought on the kicking team. The ball was snapped to holder

"God put us on this earth to be of value to others. That value is not measured by Super Bowl rings or bank accounts, but by the love we show to others."

MEL BLOUNT
Former Cornerback
Pittsburgh Steelers

Chris Gardocki—then Gardocki shocked the Bengals by pitching the ball to Dawson, who dashed around the left end for a touchdown.

But this wasn't the first time Dawson had made a major stir in football. While at the University of Texas in Austin, he built a reputation for kicking game-winning field goals, including a 50-yarder into the wind to beat Virginia 17-16 in 1995. He made that kick a week after turning down an invitation to be on *Playboy's* "All-America Team." Why did he refuse the honor? Because Dawson, a member of Fellowship of Christian Athletes, believed that accepting the *Playboy* honor would undermine his Christian testimony. After announcing his decision, he received 600 letters of support. One was from a man in an Oklahoma prison.

"I wake up without my family and my freedom each day," wrote the inmate, "all for a compromise in the right thing to do. You have set an example . . . to make the decision for what is right." After reading those words, Dawson said, "To hear someone who's in prison say they know they messed up, that they wouldn't be there if they had stood up for what they believed, and that you made them think about it, that's very special."

TEAR DOWN BARRIERS

Another way players give back is by demolishing racial barriers. When 49ers guard Guy McIntyre moved to Green Bay, he found a friend in offensive tackle Ken Ruettgers. Some would think them an unlikely pair: McIntyre is a liberal African-American from Georgia; Ruettgers is a conservative white from southern California. But McIntyre and Ruettgers have something in common that transcends all differences: their shared commitment to Jesus Christ.

Guy McIntyre

"His being white and my being black," says McIntyre, "we had a chance to talk about a lot of things. I could help him understand how the majority of black people view things."

"I found out things I had no idea about," adds Ruettgers, "especially the racism he deals with. He let me ask honest questions. He had a joy and a grace about him. A joy in the Lord."

Wide receiver Bill Brooks of the Colts, Bills, and Redskins agrees that the gospel of Jesus Christ is the key to building racial harmony. "In Galatians 3:26-28," he says, "we are told that among people who believe in Jesus 'there is neither Jew nor Greek, slave nor free, male nor female, for you are all one in Christ Jesus.' If we love God, we are not going to question God about how He made us—whether black, white, woman, male, people in Europe, people in North America, people in the Western Hemisphere. He created us all."

A VEHICLE TO TOUCH LIVES

Running back Curtis Martin of the New York Jets was raised by an industrious single mother, Rochella Martin. She worked two or three jobs at a time to make sure that young Curtis had food on the table and decent shoes on his feet. Because of her sacrifice, Curtis always knew he was loved. "I really respect her for that," he says today. "She's so hard-working. She's such a strong woman from what she's been through."

One of the jobs Rochella Martin worked was as the proprietor of Rochella's New and Used Clothing store in the Homewood section of Pittsburgh. She worried every day about being robbed and killed, and leaving young Curtis alone in the world. "But when you're in an area and you can't do any better," she said, "you have to keep going and pray and hope you return home. I would ask God, 'Please let us meet back here today.' "

Curtis grew up amid violence and tragedy. "I've seen a lot of bad things happen," he recalls. "I've seen a lot of death. I've seen a lot of people killed." Growing up in inner-city Pittsburgh, he had a fatalistic view of life. His grandmother and an aunt were both stabbed to death, and one of his best friends was shot to death.

"I know what it is to have a mentality that says this is my outcome in life," he reflects. "I knew at some time something's going to happen to me, just because you see it so much. You could be the most innocent person, and it can grab you and say, 'This is what you've been dealt in life. You're going to die like everyone else has died.' . . . I came so close so many times that I knew I'm not just lucky to be alive. I didn't know anything about God or Jesus, but I said there's something, some reason why I'm protected."

Like many Christian players, Curtis Martin sees the game as "a vehicle to touch many lives." He visits troubled kids in the detention centers in Pittsburgh. He mentors them, encouraging them in their schoolwork. He talks to kids about a relationship with Jesus Christ, and he is active in his church. Curtis Martin gives back—big time. "I believe the athlete chooses whether he'll be a positive or negative role model," he says. "I don't like any negativity. That's why I try to speak to kids as often as I can."

HOW ABOUT YOU?

Here's how some other NFL stars are giving back:

Place kicker Fuad Reveiz (Dolphins, Vikings), who comes from Colombia in South America, quietly volunteers time and money to such organizations as Habitat for Humanity and Urban Hope, Reggie White's inner-city development project. He says, "I try to follow what St. Francis of Assisi said: 'Preach the gospel each and every day—and if you have to, use words.' . . . I don't believe we're here just to make the maximum profit we can get. We're here instead to announce and proclaim God's love."

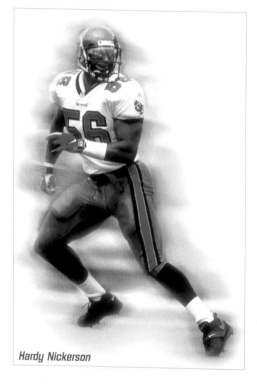

Hardy Nickerson

One of the ways football players give back is by opening their checkbooks. When Reggie White founded the Community Development Bank as a way of giving inner-city people economic opportunities, he wrote a check from his own bank account for a cool million. And when running back Barry Sanders was signed by the Detroit Lions in 1989, there was a lot of controversy about his $6.1 million, five-year contract—which included a signing bonus of $2.1 million. Some called Sanders "greedy" for taking that bonus. Yet the first thing he did was to write a check for $210,000—one-tenth of his bonus—to his home church in Wichita, Kansas.

Linebacker Hardy Nickerson (Steelers, Bucs, and Jaguars) came up from the mean streets of Compton, near Los Angeles. "I had the basic inner-city influences such as gang affiliation," he recalls, "and there was drug dealing going on. . . . I could have been right in the middle of all that stuff, but it was by the grace of God that I wasn't. He directed my path and sheltered me." Nickerson became a Christian during his teenage years, though it wasn't until the spring of 1990—well into his NFL career—that he truly dedicated his life to God.

Today, Hardy Nickerson is making a difference in the lives of inner-city youth. Soon after signing with Tampa Bay, he organized the Hardy Boys and Girls Club for underprivileged kids. He also volunteers with Tampa's Get On Board program, speaking to kids about staying in school and off of drugs. Through the Hardy Nickerson Foundation, he has created numerous educational, developmental, and mentoring programs for at-risk young people.

How about you? Even if you are not a professional athlete, you have been blessed by God. You have gifts you can use to help others. You have a platform to spread the message of Jesus Christ—your business, your ministry, your hobby, or your recreational pastime. Whatever you have, give it back to God, to your community, and to the people around you.

You've been given so much. What will you give back?

America's coach . . .
THE LIFE AND FAITH OF TOM LANDRY

For Thomas Wade Landry, coaching in the NFL started out as more of a hobby than a career. A successful Dallas insurance man, Tom Landry saw himself as a businessman—not a professional coach. During his pro football career in the early 1950s, he had seen coaches come and go, and he considered the coaching profession "too insecure."

Born in Mission, Texas, Landry flew thirty WWII combat missions with the Eighth Air Force and survived a crash landing in France. He played cornerback for one season with the old New York Yankees of the All-American Football Conference. After the Yankees merged with the NFL Giants, Landry played six more seasons with the Giants. Later, coach Jim Lee Howell put Landry in charge of the defense. In the off-season, Landry would return to Dallas and run his insurance agency.

In 1959, he signed on as the first coach of the Dallas Cowboys. In their opening season, the Cowboys failed to win a single game. Landry later joked that the team was so bad that quarterback Eddie LeBaron used to signal fair catch before taking the snap. The Cowboys suffered non-winning records until 1966, when they soared to 10-3-1. That turnaround garnered Landry the Coach of the Year honors. It marked the first of twenty consecutive winning seasons for the Cowboys.

Despite the winning records, the late '60s were marked by adversity and frustration for Tom Landry. The '66 season ended when Green Bay defeated the Cowboys in the NFL Championship game; the Packers went on to win Super Bowl I. The next season ended at the infamous Ice Bowl, when Green Bay beat Dallas on Bart Starr's last-second QB sneak; the Packers went on to win Super Bowl II.

The next two seasons, the Cowboys were eliminated in the playoffs by Cleveland. "Those two seasons," Landry said, "were the most miserable, toughest coaching years I had. When you take a good team demoralized by defeat in big games and have to turn them around, it's the toughest coaching job you can face." But those years of frustration also solidified Landry's determination to build a championship team.

The Cowboys arrived at Super Bowl V at the end of the 1970 season. Though Dallas led the Baltimore Colts 13-6 at the half, the game was decided by a 32-yard Colts

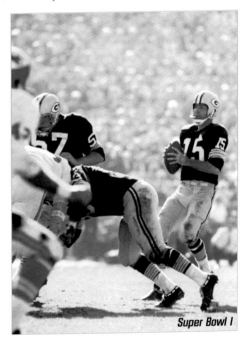

Super Bowl I

field goal. As the ball sailed through the uprights, Cowboys defensive tackle Bob Lilly groaned and tossed his helmet thirty yards downfield. As was his style, Landry showed little emotion, but the 16-13 loss was painful. Asked if it was a worse loss than previous years' losses, he replied, "You don't measure disappointment."

During those years of frustration, Tom Landry sought God's will for his life. "I reevaluated what my life purpose was," he said. "I felt God was calling me to coach." After nearly three decades of coaching, he finished his course with a record of thirteen division titles, five trips to the Super Bowl (two wins, three losses), a place in the Hall of Fame, and a career record of 270-178-6.

Tom Landry

The Cowboys' glory days began with the '71 season, capped by a 24-3 rout over the Miami Dolphins in Super Bowl VI. That championship established the Cowboys as an elite team, and it wasn't long before the Cowboys were known as "America's Team."

Tom Landry's image was all-business. Running back Walt Garrison was once asked if he ever saw Coach Landry smile. "Nope," said Garrison, "but then, I was only there for nine years." A commanding presence on the sidelines, he stood with his arms folded, watching with his angular jaw set in determination. He wore a jacket and tie and snap-brim hat—we'll never forget that trademark hat! He was a chessmaster who devised complex strategies and multiple formations, and always looked three or four plays ahead.

The cornerstone of Tom Landry's life was his faith—an abiding faith in God and a serene confidence in his own coaching ability. He possessed that paradoxical mixture of confidence and humility that is the mark of a mature Christian. He continually talked to his players about setting priorities: God, family, and team, in that order. His faith carried him through every storm of adversity, including his final battle with leukemia. On February 12, 2000, at age seventy-five, the founding coach of the Dallas Cowboys passed from this life into eternity.

The paradox of Tom Landry's coaching career is that he was great because football was *not* his number one priority. "I'm a Christian," he once observed. "That's the first thing in my life." He chose the coaching profession *not* because of an overriding passion for football, but because he felt God had called him to coach. He wanted to be wherever God wanted him to be, giving it his all.

When God called, America's coach answered.

CHAPTER EIGHT

Touchdown!

". . . Nor do I count my life dear to myself, so that I may finish my race with joy, and the ministry which I received from the Lord Jesus, to testify to the gospel of the grace of God."

ACTS 20:24

The goal in football is to score touchdowns. But what is the goal of your life?

When he played wide receiver for the New England Patriots, Irving Fryar would sometimes disappear for days, bingeing on cocaine. In 1986, during a home game against the Bills, he left the field with an injury; instead of returning to the sidelines after being treated, he went to his car, drove away from the stadium, and crashed into a tree. In 1988, the police stopped him and found a rifle in his car, loaded with hollow-point ammunition.

For much of his life, Irving Fryar was a tragedy waiting to happen. Raised in Mount Holly, New Jersey, he hung out with the G-Town gang (the G stood for ghetto). Fryar's mother was a devout Christian. His father sang in a traveling gospel group but was a heavy drinker who sometimes came home raging and violent.

"I thought that's how all families were," Fryar reflects today. "I never thought anything was wrong with mine."

What young Irving Fryar saw in his father soured him on the Christian faith. "Church didn't mean anything to me," he recalls. "Not when you'd see people act one way in church and another at home." At age thirteen, he was introduced to marijuana—by his uncle. In high school, he learned he could vent his rage on the football field without getting arrested.

Landing a football scholarship to Nebraska, Fryar distinguished himself as one of the best receivers in college football. It was no surprise that the Patriots made him their first draft pick. In Fryar, New England had a world-class wide receiver, but the team lacked a comparable quarterback. Fryar played nine seasons in New England, matched with nine different quarterbacks. As he lamented to *Sports Illustrated*, "It wasn't any use. The ball just wasn't going to get there."

In January 1986, Fryar showed up for the AFC championship game with a deep cut on his right hand—a kitchen accident, he said. But the *Boston Globe* reported that he was injured in a fight with his wife, Jacqui. Fryar missed that game but played in Super Bowl XX—a 46-10 loss to the Chicago Bears. Two days after the

Super Bowl, Fryar was in the headlines for alleged drug use. "I have a name for those years," Fryar says sadly. "The Mess."

He didn't start to pull out of The Mess until the spring of 1990. That's when his daughter Adrianne was born. She came into the world with severe heart problems, requiring open-heart surgery. Suddenly, Fryar had to focus on someone other than himself, and he decided to get clean and sober for his daughter's sake. He kept his pledge for a number of months.

Irving Fryar

One night in October, he went to a nightclub in Providence with Patriots teammate Hart Lee Dykes. There, Dykes got into an argument. The argument moved outside and became a brawl. Fryar went to his car, grabbed a pistol, and stuck it in his boot. Returning, he found Dykes sprawled on the sidewalk. As Fryar bent to help him, somebody whacked Fryar on the head with a baseball bat, gashing his scalp and knocking him cold.

The police arrived and found Irving Fryar with a pistol in his boot. They took him to jail, where he languished without medical attention until morning (the scalp wound later required eight stitches). Sitting in jail with an oozing skull, Fryar hit bottom. He considered suicide, but then he thought, *What about God?* He decided to look up a church he had heard about, the Greater Love Tabernacle in the Roxbury section of Boston. After his release, he started attending there. The preacher invited any who needed salvation to come forward and receive Jesus Christ. Irving went forward and made the biggest reception of his life.

"I had to give up and go up front and confess my sins and give my life to Christ," he recalls. "And He just knocked me out. He knocked me on the floor. The Spirit was on me. And in me. And through me."

The change that came over Irving Fryar was astounding. Over the next two years, he studied to become a preacher—and what a preacher! He works up such a sweat that his suit is drenched at the end of each service. "I'm a lot more tired after I preach," says Fryar, "than after a football game." He recalls that he first felt called to preach at seventeen, but he not only ignored that call, he *ran* from it. But when he stopped running and started living for Jesus, his life caught fire—and so did his football career.

Three years after his conversion experience, the Patriots traded Fryar to Miami. No longer did he wait in vain for the pass to arrive. Suddenly, he was a favorite target of the legendary Dan Marino. From then on, his stats began to soar. And after ten lean years in the NFL, the honors and Pro Bowl invitations began rolling in.

In 1996, Fryar moved to the Philadelphia Eagles, where he teamed with quarterback Rodney Peete. He became the first player to accrue 1,000 receiving yards with three different teams. He tried to retire to a

TV sports desk in Philly, but the Washington Redskins made him an offer he couldn't refuse. As a Redskin, Irving Fryar provides veteran leadership and role modeling for the team's talented rookie receivers.

During the football season, Irving Fryar still preaches, but the stadium is his church, and the end zone is his pulpit. He is still in the touchdown business, and every time he reaches the end zone, he waves off the cheers from the fans and points toward heaven. Why? "To let people know it's not me," he says. "It's God who saved me, who allowed me to be on the field and do the things I am able to do."

The goal of everything he says and does is Jesus Christ alone. Like the apostle Paul, Fryar can say, "Not that I have already attained, or am already perfected; but I press on, that I may lay hold of that for which Christ Jesus has also laid hold of me" (Phil. 3:12). Fryar says that because of his past, more people are open to believing his message. He explains, "I've been through the fire and I've come out as pure gold."

"I WANTED SOMETHING HE HAD"

Touchdown! Knowing Christ, having your life changed by Him, is the ultimate end zone experience. Of course, you don't have to have a problem with drugs or some other big issue in your life in order to see your need for Christ. We all need Jesus Christ. All. No exceptions. Why? Because "all have sinned and fall short of the glory of God" (Rom. 3:23).

Just ask Oakland Raiders quarterback Rich Gannon. He's never had a problem with drinking or drugs or brawling in bars. He was raised in a religious home, attended church every Sunday, and went to parochial school. In time, it came to him that his decisions about religion were really being made for him by his parents—they were not authentically *his* decisions.

Rich Gannon

After Gannon became a quarterback in the NFL, the trappings of success dulled the emptiness inside him—at least for a while. "I'd always wanted to play in the National Football League," he says. "When I finally got there, it wasn't anything like I expected. I had fame, I had the money, I had a new home and a car . . . but I realized there was an emptiness in my heart."

Gannon was drafted in 1987 by the Patriots, then dealt off to the Vikings a mere two weeks later. There, he patrolled the sidelines as Wade Wilson's backup, making good money but seeing no action. One night, he attended a Vikings chapel service. "I heard a speaker give his testimony," he recalls. "I felt so guilty inside because he had been wounded in Vietnam, and physically he was broken. He was missing an arm, a leg, and an eye. . . . I had basically everything. But I felt I wanted something he had. I knew what he had was that inner joy and peace that a relationship with Jesus brings."

Gannon stayed after the chapel service and talked to chaplain Tom Lamphere. He thought it over, then decided to place his trust in Jesus Christ. That decision gave him the first lasting peace he had ever known.

In 1990, Rich Gannon became the starter. Then, in '93, the Vikings made Jim McMahon their top signal-caller, and Gannon was sent to the Redskins, where he backed up Mark Rypien. After a year in Washington, he was sidelined by a rotator cuff injury and cut from the team. He wondered if he would ever play again.

"I never prayed to the Lord that He'd put me back in the National Football League," says Gannon. "I just prayed for guidance and strength—that He would take control of my life." He returned to Minneapolis, worked with a telecommunications company, and let his right shoulder heal.

In the spring of '95, he got the call he'd been waiting for: The Kansas City Chiefs wanted him as Steve Bono's backup. For the next three years, he wore a baseball cap instead of a football helmet, backing up first Bono, then Elvis Grbac. When Grbac was injured, he got a chance to prove himself in sixteen games in '97 and '98. His performance attracted the attention of Raiders coach Jon Gruden, and in March 1999, Gannon signed a four-year contract with Oakland.

"In Christ, I know that I have Someone who loves me regardless of how much money I make, how many touchdowns I score, or the status I do or do not have. He loves me regardless, and He'll never leave me."

GLYN MILBURN
Running Back, Detroit Lions, Denver Broncos, Chicago Bears

Rich Gannon brings a unique approach to the game. Unlike your classic drop-back, stand-in-the-pocket, throw-a-perfect-spiral quarterback, Rich Gannon makes plays on the run. His style is not always pretty. In fact, television analyst and ex-QB Phil Simms says Gannon's approach can be downright ugly. "Rich Gannon drops back, runs to the right, stops, runs to the left, throws it underhand or throws it sidearm and the ball wobbles a little bit," says Simms—yet he says it not as a criticism but as the highest praise. Rich Gannon makes plays any way he can.

During the 2000 season, Gannon led the Raiders to the AFC championship game. There, Ravens defensive tackle Tony Siragusa drove Gannon into the ground with a full-body slam. Gannon left the game with a dislocated shoulder, and the 340-pound Siragusa was later fined $10,000 for the illegal hit. The Ravens went on to win that game and Super Bowl XXXV. But Rich Gannon had proven himself a playoff contender.

"One thing I've noticed," he reflects, "is that the most disciplined, the most prepared, the most consistent guys you can count on in this business are Christians. That's not to say that other guys who aren't Christians aren't professional. But the guys who have a relationship with the Lord are able to set aside the distractions of everyday life, and they are able to focus and concentrate. They have their personal lives in order, so they can put all the nonsense aside and focus on their job."

In April 1995, offensive tackle Tony Boselli was drafted by the expansion Jacksonville Jaguars. Fresh out of USC and recently married to his college sweetheart, Angi, he arrived at training camp and soon befriended the man he would be protecting in the pocket, quarterback Mark Brunell. Meanwhile, Angi and Brunell's wife, Stacy, became good friends and began a Bible study together.

One evening, Brunell invited the young couple to his home to hear Bible teacher Greg Ball give a talk. While there, they listened to Greg tell of God's grace and what it means to have Jesus Christ as the Lord of your life. When Ball asked if anyone wanted to receive Jesus as Lord, Boselli felt a tug inside. "I stood up that night, not knowing what I was doing," Boselli recalls. "I just knew that something was missing— something I was lacking—and that was to know the Creator. Unless you know the Creator, you don't know why you were put here, and you don't know your purpose here on this earth."

Tony Boselli will tell you that the Christian life is a challenging life. It's hard, it takes discipline, but he wouldn't have it any other way. "It's an everyday thing," he says. "I've got to wake up and say, 'Jesus, you're my Lord. . . . I submit to your authority and what you say goes.' . . . I struggle every day, and I have to rely on the grace of God to get me through the day."

A RADICAL CHANGE

Qadry Ismail is the younger half of the NFL's Dynamic Duo, Raghib "Rocket" Ismail and Qadry "Missile" Ismail. Both are wide receivers—Raghib with the Dallas Cowboys and Qadry with the Baltimore Ravens. And both have the speed of a high-velocity projectile; hence the nicknames.

Before landing in Baltimore, Qadry bounced around the NFL for a while—Vikings, Packers, Dolphins, Saints. His best pre-Ravens season was in '94, when he caught 45 passes for 696 yards and 5 touchdowns with the Vikings. But his football career seemed cloudy in '97 and '98—back-to-back seasons in which he didn't make a single reception. Cut by the Saints, it looked as though his NFL career was over.

In the '99 off-season, Qadry Ismail sat on the porch of his home in Boca Raton, Florida, and prayed for direction. As he prayed, he sensed the presence and the answer of God. Only a short time later, he received a call from coach Brian Billick of the Ravens. Billick had coached Ismail in Minnesota and knew that the Missile was a dangerous receiver with blinding speed after the catch. Despite Ismail's reputation for inconsistency, Billick believed that Ismail could make a big contribution. So God answered Qadry's prayer, and the Missile became a nuclear-grade weapon in the Baltimore arsenal.

His first season as a Raven, the Missile soared, rolling up 1,105 yards on 68 receptions, with 6 touchdowns. The following year, he was not only a major factor in getting the Ravens to Super Bowl XXXV, but a 44-yard Dilfer-to-Ismail hookup was the longest pass play of the game.

Qadry's success, however, came after a long journey to faith. He was born to a Muslim family. His father, Ibrahim, died when Qadry was nine. His mother, Fatma, supported three boys by herself—Raghib, Qadry, and youngest brother Sulaiman—plus a daughter from a previous marriage. They lived in a dangerous Newark housing project, surrounded by crime and drugs. Fatma loved her kids and worried about their safety. So, tearfully and reluctantly, Fatma sent the kids to live with their grandmother, Laura Bauknight, in Wilkes-Barre.

Qadry Ismail

Grandma Bauknight was a Christian. For a while, the contrast between the religion of his mother and the religion of his grandmother confused young Qadry. "I was always going back and forth," he recalls, "between my religion and my grandmother's. I was being rebellious toward my grandmother, but I would listen to her. I realized the God I was serving, Allah, wasn't real to me, because I didn't feel him when I prayed to him. I knew that the God my grandmother served, Jesus Christ, was very much real. She got results and answers. That moved me to go to the God who loves and cares about you, to know Him on a personal basis."

Looking back on his checkered NFL career, Qadry says, "My life on the field has never been easy. I think a lot of times people think once you get the Lord, you've got everything handed to you. But that's not the case. Sometimes you're even more persecuted than before. Like it says in my favorite verse in the Bible, James 1:2-4: 'My brethren, count it all joy when you fall into various trials, knowing that the testing of your faith produces patience. But let patience have its perfect work, that you may be perfect and complete, lacking nothing.'"

Chris Sanders

That's what it means to score a "touchdown" in the game of life. It means overcoming the obstacles and adversity of this life, connecting with God through faith in Jesus Christ, and arriving in the end zone of His power, love, and grace. Do you know the sweet victory of knowing Christ? If you do, then you know a thrill of victory that is higher than any Lambeau leap, greater than any Mile High salute.

Sunday is a special day for the men of the NFL. Sunday is a special day for the fans who love this game. Everything happens on Sunday. That's when the game is played. That's when the victories are won. And, of course, there's Super Bowl Sunday—the biggest Sunday of all.

But even a Super Bowl victory pales in importance next to the triumph that took place one Sunday morning, some 2,000 years ago. As former quarterback Roger Staubach of the Dallas Cowboys once put it, "As a Christian I believe Jesus Christ died for our sins on that Friday, that He came back from the dead on Sunday, and His resurrection gives us a chance for everlasting life. . . . We have our temporary joys and sorrows, for which there are temporary solutions. The permanent solution is that relationship with Christ. That is the bond which extends beyond this earth."

Resurrection Sunday was a Sunday like no other, before or since. What happened on that incredible Sunday, when Jesus exploded from the tomb in resurrection power, still sends shock waves around the world. It still impacts men and transforms lives. For those who have made Jesus their Lord and Master, the Resurrection is something that happens not just on Sunday, but every day of the week, every week of the year.

Knowing Christ is not just the thrill of a lifetime. It's a touchdown in eternity. And there's nothing in this world more exciting than that!

In the zone . . .

FOOTBALL GREATS TALK ABOUT THEIR FAITH

Here's how some NFL stars, past and present, describe their own spiritual touchdown experience:

Broncos cornerback **Terrell Buckley**: "If you had asked me if I wanted a Super Bowl ring or wanted to be saved before I was saved, I would have had to think about it. Now it's not even a decision. . . . I'm just trying to enjoy every minute, every hour, every day, every situation. Tomorrow's not promised us, and I let the Lord lead my life. Life is ten percent what happens to me and ninety percent how I react to it."

Former defensive tackle **Dave Rowe**, Oakland Raiders, remembering Super Bowl XI: "I knocked down three passes, caused a fumble, and recovered a fumble. We won 32-14. As soon as the game ended, the team went to pick up Coach John Madden, but I ran to the locker room because I knew the first ones in were more likely to get interviewed on TV. So Tom Brookshier put the mike in my face and said, 'This has got to be the greatest moment in your life.' I said to Tom, 'No, this is not the greatest moment in my life, but I sure thank my Lord and Savior Jesus Christ for allowing me to play.' That was in 1977, when very few people would profess their spirituality on TV. You just didn't say it. But hundreds of people have come up to me and said, 'I'll never forget when you said that.' "

Kicker **Jason Hanson**, Detroit Lions: "Football is so temporary. The money, the fame, all of that. Yet your relationship with Christ, that's life. I want people to know that's what life is about. I want people to know that my life is centered around Jesus Christ."

Former quarterback **Jim Zorn**, Seahawks 1976-84: "My relationship with Christ continues to strengthen as I get to know Him better through Bible study, prayer, conversation, and being challenged by others."

Former defensive tackle **Chad Hennings**, Dallas Cowboys: "It was just a few weeks after Super Bowl XXX in Phoenix that our son, Chase, became ill. His illness and the difficulty of seeing him struggle was the greatest challenge that Tammy and I have faced. That illness came just days after the two sacks and our Super Bowl victory. . . . Through the great times and the difficult times, God desires to build character—the character of his Son, Jesus Christ—in us."

Junior Seau

Linebacker **Junior Seau**, San Diego Chargers: "The Bible is the rock and the base of our being. Without God and His Word, which He has left us, there isn't any answer."

Kicker **Adam Vinatieri**, New England Patriots: "God answered my prayers, drew me closer to himself, and led me to people who are helping me accomplish my goals in life as well as in football. As I have asked God for help, received His forgiveness and read the Bible more in depth, He has more than met my needs."

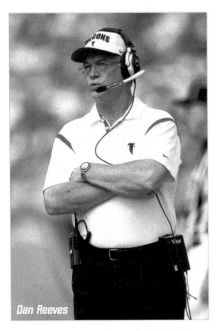

Dan Reeves

Broncos offensive lineman **Mark Schlereth**, after suffering a herniated disc: "The world said, 'You've been through sixteen knee surgeries, you must be one tough son of a gun,' and I really believed it. I really believed I was this tough hombre who could play through anything. But this back thing showed me I could boast in nothing, that God is in complete control. Medically, I should not be playing. It's just a miracle of God."

Falcons head coach (and former Cowboys halfback) **Dan Reeves**: "God doesn't take sides, but He is with you whether you win or lose—in good times and in bad. . . . A knee injury ended my professional career as a running back. But what seemed tragic was a blessing. Two years later I was asked to be a player-coach and entered into a profession in which I thought I had no interest. God has a wonderful plan for our lives."

Former defensive tackle **Roosevelt "Rosey" Grier**, N.Y. Giants and L.A. Rams (and the man who subdued the killer of Robert F. Kennedy in Los Angeles, 1968): "I look back on my life—the things I've done, the people I've known and cared about—but as wonderful as all of that is, it doesn't begin to compare to the moment I came to know Jesus Christ as my Savior."

Punter **Josh Bidwell**, reflecting on his battle with cancer: "Knowing God was working in my life at the time—that was the biggest comfort I've had in my entire life. I didn't know if I was going to live or die, but I knew I was in good hands. God entrusted me with this to glorify Him, and I didn't want to waste that. I know God has a wonderful plan for me. My only duty is to keep my focus on Him."

Running back **Byron Hanspard**, Atlanta Falcons: "I won't promise that if you get saved your life will be perfect. You will still have trials and tribulations. I've had my share already in the NFL. But I can guarantee you that God will be your guide, your peace, and your joy."

ACKNOWLEDGMENTS

I would like to acknowledge the following people for their effort, support, and encouragement of the writing of this book:

Thanks to Jim Denney, longtime collaborator and friend, for his work in hammering my thoughts and ideas into a readable structure; and to my friends Jack Countryman, Jonathan Merkh, and Jenny Baumgartner for turning a black-and-white manuscript into a book of vivid color and visual power.

Special thanks to Bob Vander Weide, president and CEO of RDV Sports, and the entire RDV Sports family; my assistant Melinda Ethington—thank you for your commitment and hard work; Leslie Boucher and Hank Martens of the mailroom and copy room at RDV Sports—your willingness to always help me out is appreciated.

A big thank-you goes to my proofreaders/fact-checkers/critics: to my longtime friend Ken Hussar; and to Seymour Siwoff of the New York-based Elias Sports Bureau, the nation's premier processor of sports statistics.

My thanks to Dave Branon of *Sports Spectrum* magazine for time spent researching and providing material for this book. All quotations from *Sports Spectrum* are used by permission. *Sports Spectrum,* a Christian sports magazine, Grand Rapids, MI. For subscription information, call 1-800-283-8333.

And thanks to David Smale and Debbie Snow of the Fellowship of Christian Athletes World Headquarters, 8701 Leeds Road, Kansas City, MO 64129, for time spent researching and providing material for this book. All quotations from the Fellowship of Christian Athletes' *Sharing the Victory* magazine are used by permission. For subscription information, call 1-800-289-0909.

And as always, special thanks to my wife, Ruth, for her partnership and support in everything I do.

Grateful acknowledgments for quotations included in this book are made to the following:

Armour, Justin. "Armoured and Ready," by Will Greer. Fellowship of Christian Athletes' *Sharing the Victory*, December 1998, p. 10.

Bidwell, Josh. "Bidwell delivers message of faith," author unavailable, August 14, 2000, was electronically retrieved at http://www.packers.com/community/news/000714bidwellgolf.html.

Blount, Mel. "Leaderboard," author not available, *Sports Spectrum*, July-August 1991, p. 12.

Boselli, Tony. "To Protect and Serve," by Buddy Shacklette, *Sports Spectrum*, December 1999, pp. 18ff.

Boulware, Peter. "We helped each other make wise choices," by Peter Boulware with Roxanne Robbins, *Sports Spectrum*, November 1998, p. 4.

Brooks, Bill. "Breaking the Race Barrier," by Bill Brooks, *Sports Spectrum*, January 1995, p. 25.

Brown, Reggie. "Lions and Christians," by Lorraine Kee and Robert Grossman, *The Nation*, August 10, 1998, pp. 37-38; "A life is preserved," by Dennis Dillon, *The Sporting News*, March 23, 1998, pp. 22ff.; "Doctors: Brown got fast, effective care," by Jarrett Bell, *USA Today*, December 23, 1997, p. 1C.

Brunell, Mark. "Air Apparent," by Ken Walker, *Sports Spectrum*, September 1997, p. 15.

Buckley, Terrell. "Newcomer Buckley Leads Broncos' Air Defense," author not available, November 9, 2000, was electronically retrieved at http://www.denverbroncos.com.

Burrough, John (on Eugene Robinson). "Mr. Relevant," by David Moriah, *Sports Spectrum*, January-February 2000, pp. 18ff.

Carter, Cris. "Cris Carter proud to win Payton prize," by Kent Youngblood, *Minneapolis Star Tribune*, January 29, 2000, p. 10C; "Cris Carter Knows What's Most Important," by Will Greer, Fellowship of Christian Athletes' *Sharing the Victory*, December 1997, pp. 7-8.

Conwell, Ernie. "Warner's Brothers," player interviews (Ernie Conwell et al.), *Sports Spectrum*, July-August 2000, p. 14.

Cunningham, Randall. "A Time to Heal," by Roxanne Robbins, *Sports Spectrum*, December 1997, p. 21.

Dawson, Phil. "Keeping the faith," by Bill Nichols, *The Dallas Morning News*, September 26, 1996, p. 1B.

Dilfer, Trent. "Trent Dilfer: Reaching beyond adversity," by Andy Boogaard, *The Fresno Bee*, January 14, 2001, pp. D1,D5; "Dilfer's confidence lifts team," by Kathy Orton, *The Washington Post*, November 16, 2000, p. D6; "Super Bowl XXXV: Talk of the Town," by Michael Silver, *Sports Illustrated*, February 5, 2001, pp. 44ff.; "Dilfer: 'I've never felt anything this good,' " by Michael Wilbon and Kathy Orton, *The Washington Post*, January 29, 2001, p. D13.

Dungy, Tony. "The Long Road Back," by Gwen Diaz, *Sports Spectrum*, January 1997, p. 15.

Elliss, Luther. "Luther Elliss," by Rob Bentz, *Sports Spectrum*, November-December 2000, p. 21.

Esiason, Boomer (on Mike Singletary). "NFL: Football's 100 Greatest Players: The Hit Men," by Phil Barber, *The Sporting News*, November 1, 1999, p. 13.

Fryar, Irving. "Didn't you used to be Irving Fryar?," by Victor Lee, *Sports Spectrum*, January 1994, pp. 28ff.; "Fryar and Brimstone," by Rick Reilly, *Sports Illustrated*, June 5, 1995, pp. 82ff.; "Reborn a Redskin: Fryar learns it's better to give than just to receive," by Bob Cohn, *The Washington Times*, September 5, 1999, p. A1.

Gannon, Rich. "Out of Nowhere," by Dave Branon and Paul Johnson, *Sports Spectrum*, January-February 2001, pp. 26ff.

Gibbs, Joe. "A Guy Named Joe," by Caron Pappas Myers, *Sports Spectrum*, NASCAR 1997 issue, pp. 22-23.

Gilbert, Sean. "Rams' Gilbert now playing for 'eternal prize'," by Bernie Miklasz, *St. Louis Post-Dispatch*, May 8, 1995, p. 1C; "Many athletes have religion, violent game in their lives," by Steve Reed, *Gaston Gazette*, December 23, 1999, was electronically retrieved at http://www.gastongazette.com/panthersnews/_article/00000154.html.

Green, Darrell. "Intercepting the City," by Allen Palmeri, *Sports Spectrum*, January 1995, pp. 28ff.; "Green, 40, signs 5-year deal with the 'Skins," author not available, *The Toronto Star*, May 31, 2000, electronically retrieved at www.elibrary.com.

Grier, Rosey. "Building a Winning Team," by Kathi Mills, Fellowship of Christian Athletes' *Sharing the Victory*, October 1990, p. 15.

Griese, Brian. Personal interview with Brian Griese.

Hanson, Jason. "Leaderboard," author not available, *Sports Spectrum*, December 1993, p. 20.

Hanspard, Byron. "Straight Talk with Byron Hanspard," by Byron Hanspard and Ken Walker, *Sports Spectrum*, January-February 2000, p. 31.

Ismail, Qadry. "Guided Missile," by Richard Dunn, *Sports Spectrum*, December 1995, pp. 28-30.

Jackson, Keith. "Leaderboard," author not available, *Sports Spectrum*, January 1995, p. 12.

Kaufman, Napoleon. "Victory" by Napoleon Kaufman with Paul Johnson, *Sports Spectrum*, December 1997, p. 19.

Landry, Tom. "Coach Tom Landry Dies," by Bart Barnes, *The Washington Post*, February 13, 2000, p. A1; "Building America's Team," by David Moore, *The Dallas Morning News*, February 13, 2000, p. 31A; "The essence of an era," by Blackie Sherrod, *The Dallas Morning News*, February 14, 2000, p. 10F.

Lloyd, Greg. "The greatest linebacker in football history . . . ," by Rick Telander, *Sports Illustrated*, September 6, 1993, pp. 54ff.

McIntyre, Guy. "The Odd Couple," by Rob Bentz, *Sports Spectrum*, January 1996, pp. 9ff.

Martin, Curtis. "Patriot Games," by Ray Fittipaldo, *Sports Spectrum*, September 1996, p. 21; "Martin always elusive," by Randy Lange, *The Bergen Record*, August 23, 1998, p. S1.

Maryland, Russell. "Man at Work," by John Weber and Jim Gibbs, *Sports Spectrum*, January 1994, p. 15.

Metzelaars, Pete. "Putting Family First," author unavailable, *Sports Spectrum*, Super Bowl 1997, p. 23.

Michels, John. "Exemploids," by John Michels with Roxanne Robbins, *Sports Spectrum*, January-February 1999, p. 2.

Muñoz, Anthony. "Hold that line!," by Ken Walker, *Sports Spectrum*, January-February 1992, pp. 18ff.

Nickerson, Hardy. "Head of the Club," by Heath Lynch, *Sports Spectrum*, October 1996, p. 28.

Offerdahl, John. "Real Men Eat Bagels," by Victor Lee, *Sports Spectrum*, January 1995, p. 9.

Pelfrey, Doug. "Kindness for Kids," by Allen Palmeri, Fellowship of Christian Athletes' *Sharing the Victory*, December 1999, p. 19.

Reeves, Dan. "Rocky Mountain Highs and Lows," by Ken Walker, *Sports Spectrum*, January-February 1991, pp. 23ff.

Reich, Frank. "Frank Reich's Hope is in Christ Alone," by Joe Ciffa, Fellowship of Christian Athletes' *Sharing the Victory*, November 1993, p. 7; "Past Super Bowl Players Go Beyond Football," by Victor Lee, *Sports Spectrum*, January-February 2000, p. 4; "The Comeback: Buffalo 41, Houston 38, Jan. 3, 1993," by Phil Barber, NFL Publishing, was electronically retrieved at http://nfl.com/news/mostmemorable5.html.

Reveiz, Fuad. "Leaderboard," author not available, *Sports Spectrum*, September 1996, p. 12.

Robinson, Eugene. "Packer All-Pro Free Safety Eugene Robinson," by Tim Gustafson and Tom Felton, *Sports Spectrum*, January-February 1998, pp. 18ff.

Rowe, Dave. "Past Super Bowl Players Go Beyond Football," by Victor Lee, *Sports Spectrum*, January-February 2000, p. 4.

Ruettgers, Ken. "The Odd Couple," by Rob Bentz, *Sports Spectrum*, January 1996, pp. 9ff.

Sanders, Chris. "In His Grip," by Bill Sorrell, Fellowship of Christian Athletes' *Sharing the Victory*, August-September 1999, p. 12.

Sanders, Deion. "Prime Time: Excerpts from Deion Sanders' Book," by Deion Sanders, *Sports Spectrum*, January-February 1999, p. 19.

Schlereth, Mark. "Leaderboard," Allen Palmeri, *Sports Spectrum*, January-February 1998, p. 11.

Seau, Junior. "Learning the Value of Character," by Dave Branon, Fellowship of Christian Athletes' *Sharing the Victory*, January 1998, p. 13.

Singletary, Mike. "Bearing the Truth," by Mike Sandrolini, *Sports Spectrum*, January-February 1992, pp. 13ff.; "Bear With Me," by Mike Sandrolini, *Sports Spectrum*, Super Bowl 1993, pp. 11ff.; "The greatest linebacker in football history . . . ," by Rick Telander, *Sports Illustrated*, September 6, 1993, pp. 54ff.

Smith, Darrin. "Darrin Is Rarin' to Go," by Jim Gibbs, *Sports Spectrum*, November 1993, p. 9.

Staubach, Roger. *Time Enough to Win*, by Roger Staubach with Frank Luksa (Waco, Tex.: Word Books, 1980), pp. 120, 121.

Stephenson, Dwight. "Straight talk with Dwight Stephenson," interview with Dwight Stephenson, *Sports Spectrum*, January-February 1999, p. 31.

Sports Illustrated commentary. "Point After," by Rick Reilly, *Sports Illustrated*, February 4, 1991, p. 86.

Taylor, Lawrence. "The greatest linebacker in football history . . . ," by Rick Telander, *Sports Illustrated*, September 6, 1993, pp. 54ff.

Teaff, Grant. "Bond formed during crisis stays strong," by Steve Blow, *The Dallas Morning News*, September 27, 1996, p. 31A.

Timmerman, Adam. "Rabbits' Feat," by Don Wilding, *Sports Spectrum*, January-February 1998, p. 24.

Tobeck, Robbie. "Just Say No," by John Dodderidge, Fellowship of Christian Athletes' *Sharing the Victory*, December 1998, p. 14.

Vinatieri, Adam. "Rabbits' Feat," by Don Wilding, *Sports Spectrum*, January-February 1998, p. 24.

White, Reggie. Personal interview with Reggie White; Reggie White, *In the Trenches* (Nashville: Thomas Nelson, 1996, 1st edition), pp. 11 & 23; "Man on a mission," by Johnette Howard, *Sports Illustrated*, February 1, 1997, pp. 24ff.

White, William. "White Knight," by Jeff Peek, *Sports Spectrum*, September-October 1991, p. 13.

Wilkinson, Bruce. *Experiencing Spiritual Breakthroughs* by Bruce Wilkinson (Sisters, Oreg.: Multnomah, 1999), p. 111.

Williams, Aeneas. "Staying Focused: Aeneas Williams," by Dean Jackson, Fellowship of Christian Athletes' *Sharing the Victory*, September 96, p. 7.

Williams, Jimmy. "The greatest linebacker in football history . . . ," by Rick Telander, *Sports Illustrated*, September 6, 1993, pp. 54ff.

Wuerffel, Danny. "The Sacrifice of Praise," by Danny Wuerffel, Fellowship of Christian Athletes' *Sharing the Victory*, January 1997, p. 10.

Zorn, Jim. "Catching Up With . . . ," author not available, *Sports Spectrum*, May-June 1991, p. 29.

You can contact Pat Williams directly:

Pat Williams
c/o RDV Sports
8701 Maitland Summit Boulevard
Orlando, FL 32810
(407) 916-2404
pwilliams@rdvsports.com

If you would like to set up a speaking engagement
for Pat Williams, you may write to his assistant,
Melinda Ethington, at the above address or call
her at (407) 916-2454. Requests can also be
faxed to (407) 916-2986 or e-mailed to
methington@rdvsports.com.